YOUR PERSONAL

ASTROLOGY

PLANNER

LIBRA
2010

YOUR PERSONAL
ASTROLOGY
PLANNER

LIBRA
2010

RICK LEVINE **& JEFF** JAWER

STERLING

New York / London
www.sterlingpublishing.com

STERLING and the distinctive Sterling logo are registered
trademarks of Sterling Publishing Co., Inc.

2 4 6 8 10 9 7 5 3 1

Published by Sterling Publishing Co., Inc.
387 Park Avenue South, New York, NY 10016
© 2009 Sterling Publishing Co., Inc.
Text © 2009 Rick Levine and Jeff Jawer
Distributed in Canada by Sterling Publishing
c/o Canadian Manda Group, 165 Dufferin Street,
Toronto, Ontario, Canada M6K 3H6
Distributed in the United Kingdom by GMC Distribution Services
Castle Place, 166 High Street, Lewes, East Sussex, England BN7 1XU
Distributed in Australia by Capricorn Link (Australia) Pty. Ltd.
P.O. Box 704, Windsor, NSW 2756, Australia

Sterling ISBN 978-1-4027-6408-0

For information about custom editions, special sales, premium and
corporate purchases, please contact Sterling Special Sales
Department at 800-805-5489 or
specialsales@sterlingpublishing.com.

TABLE OF CONTENTS

Introduction   7
Moon Charts   11

CHAPTER 1: ASTROLOGY, YOU & THE WORLD   15

CHAPTER 2: LIBRA AUGUST–DECEMBER   35
              2009 OVERVIEW

CHAPTER 3: 2010 HOROSCOPE   46

APPENDIXES
2010 Month-at-a-Glance Astrocalendar   131
Famous Librans   143
Libra in Love   145
Author Biographies   158
Acknowledgments   159

THE PURPOSE OF THIS BOOK

The more you learn about yourself, the better able you are to wisely use the energies in your life. For more than 3,000 years, astrology has been the sharpest tool in the box for describing the human condition. Used by virtually every culture on the planet, astrology continues to serve as a link between individual lives and planetary cycles. We gain valuable insights into personal issues with a birth chart, and can plot the patterns of the year ahead in meaningful ways for individuals as well as groups. You share your sun sign with eight percent of humanity. Clearly, you're not all going to have the same day, even if the basic astrological cycles are the same. Your individual circumstances, the specific factors of your entire birth chart, and your own free will help you write your unique story.

The purpose of this book is to describe the energies of the Sun, Moon, and planets for the year ahead and help you create your future, rather than being a victim of it. We aim to facilitate your journey by showing you the turns ahead in the road of life and hopefully the best ways to navigate them.

YOU ARE THE STAR
OF YOUR LIFE

It is not our goal to simply predict events. Rather, we are reporting the planetary energies—the cosmic weather in which you are living—so that you understand these conditions and know how to use them most effectively.

The power, though, isn't in the stars, but in your mind, your heart, and the choices that you make every day. Regardless of how strongly you are buffeted by the winds of change or bored by stagnation, you have many ways to view any situation. Learning about the energies of the Sun, Moon, and planets will both sharpen and widen your perspective, thereby giving you additional choices.

The language of astrology is a gift of awareness, not a rigid set of rules. It works best when blended with common sense, intuition, and self-trust. This is your life, and no one knows how to live it as well as you. Take what you need from this book and leave the rest. Although the planets set the stage for the year ahead, you're the writer, director, and star of your life and you can play the part in whatever way you choose. *Your Personal Astrology Planner* uses information about your sun sign to give you a better understanding of how the planetary waves will wash upon your shore. We each navigate our lives through time, and each moment has unique qualities. Astrology gives us the ability to describe the constantly changing timescape. For example, if you know the trajectory and the speed of an approaching storm, you can choose to delay a leisurely afternoon sail on the bay, thus avoiding an unpleasant situation.

By reading this book, you can improve your ability to align with the cosmic weather, the larger patterns that affect you day to day. You can become more effective by aligning with the cosmos and cocreating the year ahead with a better understanding of the energies around you.

Astrology doesn't provide quick fixes to life's complex issues. It doesn't offer neatly packed black-and-white answers in a world filled with an infinite variety of shapes and colors. It can, however, give you a much clearer picture of the invisible forces influencing your life.

ENERGY & EVENTS

Two sailboats can face the same gale yet travel in opposite directions as a result of how the sails are positioned. Similarly, how you respond to the energy of a particular set of circumstances may be more responsible for your fate than the given situation itself. We delineate the energetic winds for your year ahead, but your attitude shapes the unfolding events, and your responses alter your destiny.

This book emphasizes the positive, not because all is good, but because astrology shows us ways to transform even the power of a storm into beneficial results. Empowerment comes from learning to see the invisible energy patterns that impact the visible landscape as you fill in the details of your story every day on this spinning planet, orbited by the Moon, lit by the Sun, and colored by the nuances of the planets.

You are a unique point in an infinite galaxy of unlimited possibilities, and the choices that you make have consequences. So use this book in a most magical way to consciously improve your life.

MOON CHARTS

2010 NEW MOONS

Each New Moon marks the beginning of a cycle. In general, this is the best time to plant seeds for future growth. Use the days preceeding the New Moon to finish old business prior to starting what comes next. The focused mind can be quite sharp during this phase. Harness the potential of the New Moon by stating your intentions—out loud or in writing—for the weeks ahead. Hold these goals in your mind; help them grow to fruition through conscious actions as the Moon gains light during the following two weeks. In the chart below, the dates and times refer to when the Moon and Sun align in each zodiac sign (see p16), initiating a new lunar cycle.

DATE	TIME	SIGN
January 15	2:11 AM EST	Capricorn (ECLIPSE)
February 13	9:51 PM EST	Aquarius
March 15	5:01 PM EDT	Pisces
April 14	8:28 AM EDT	Aries
May 13	9:04 PM EDT	Taurus
June 12	7:14 AM EDT	Gemini
July 11	3:40 PM EDT	Cancer (ECLIPSE)
August 9	11:08 PM EDT	Leo
September 8	6:29 AM EDT	Virgo
October 7	2:44 PM EDT	Libra
November 6	12:51 AM EDT	Scorpio
December 5	12:35 PM EST	Sagittarius

2010 FULL MOONS

The Full Moon reflects the light of the Sun as subjective feelings reflect the objective events of the day. Dreams seem bigger; moods feel stronger. The emotional waters run with deeper currents. This is the phase of culmination, a turning point in the energetic cycle. Now it's time to listen to the inner voices. Rather than starting new projects, the two weeks after the Full Moon are when we complete what we can and slow our outward expressions in anticipation of the next New Moon. In this chart, the dates and times refer to when the moon is opposite the sun in each zodiac sign, marking the emotional peak of each lunar cycle.

DATE	TIME	SIGN
January 30	1:17 AM EST	Leo
February 28	11:37 AM EST	Virgo
March 29	10:25 PM EDT	Libra
April 28	8:18 AM EDT	Scorpio
May 27	7:07 PM EDT	Sagittarius
June 26	7:30 AM EDT	Capricorn **(ECLIPSE)**
July 25	9:36 PM EDT	Aquarius
August 24	1:04 PM EDT	Pisces
September 23	5:17 AM EDT	Aries
October 22	9:36 PM EDT	Aries
November 21	12:27 PM EST	Taurus
December 21	3:13 AM EST	Gemini **(ECLIPSE)**

ASTROLOGY, YOU & THE WORLD

WELCOME TO YOUR SUN SIGN

The Sun, Moon, and Earth and all the planets lie within a plane called the **ecliptic** and move through a narrow band of stars made up by 12 constellations called the **zodiac**. The Earth revolves around the Sun once a year, but from our point of view, it appears that the Sun moves through each sign of the zodiac for one month. There are 12 months and astrologically there are 12 signs. The astrological months, however, do not match our calendar, and start between the 19th and 23rd of each month. Everyone is born to an astrological month, like being born in a room with a particular perspective of the world. Knowing your sun sign provides useful information about your personality and your future, but for a more detailed astrological analysis, a full birth chart calculation based on your precise date, time, and place of birth is necessary. Get your complete birth chart online at:

http://www.tarot.com/astrology/astroprofile

This book is about your zodiac sign. Your Sun in the air sign of diplomatic Libra is highly sensitive to balance and harmony in relationships, which is why you're so concerned with fairness and maintaining the peace. Trying to keep other people happy is one of your gifts, even though sometimes you sacrifice too much of your own needs to make this happen. You are in your element when you connect with gracious people in attractive surroundings.

THE PLANETS

We refer to the Sun and Moon as planets. Don't worry; we do know about modern astronomy. Although the Sun is really a star and the Moon is a satellite, they are called planets for astrological purposes. The astrological planets are the Sun, the Moon, Mercury, Venus, Mars, Jupiter, Saturn, Chiron, Uranus, Neptune, and Pluto.

Your sun sign is the most obvious astrological placement, for the Sun returns to the same sign every year. But at the same time, the Moon is orbiting the Earth, changing signs every two and a third days. Mercury, Venus, and Mars each move through a sign in a few weeks to a few months.

Jupiter spends a whole year in a sign—and Pluto visits a sign for up to 30 years! The ever-changing positions of the planets alter the energetic terrain through which we travel. The planets are symbols; each has a particular range of meanings. For example, Venus is the goddess of love, but it really symbolizes beauty in a spectrum of experiences. Venus can represent romantic love, sensuality, the arts, or good food. It activates anything that we value, including personal possessions and even money. To our ancestors, the planets actually animated life on Earth. In this way of thinking, every beautiful flower contains the essence of Venus.

Each sign has a natural affinity to an individual planet, and as this planet moves through the sky, it sends messages of particular interest to people born under that sign. Venus, your key or ruling planet, is the goddess of love, beauty, pleasure and fine objects. Its movement shows where relationship and self-worth issues, the principles of attraction and desire, and money come into your life, as well as time when you're open to receiving gifts of all kinds. Planets can be described by many different words, for the mythology of each is a rich tapestry. In this book we use a variety of words when talking

about each planet in order to convey the most
applicable meaning. The table below describes a
few keywords for each planet, including the Sun
and Moon.

PLANET	SYMBOL	KEYWORDS
Sun	☉	Consciousness, Will, Vitality
Moon	☽	Subconscious, Emotions, Habits
Mercury	☿	Communication, Thoughts, Transportation
Venus	♀	Desire, Love, Money, Values
Mars	♂	Action, Physical Energy, Drive
Jupiter	♃	Expansion, Growth, Optimism
Saturn	♄	Contraction, Maturity, Responsibility
Chiron	⚷	Healing, Pain, Subversion
Uranus	♅	Awakening, Unpredictable, Inventive
Neptune	♆	Imagination, Spirituality, Confusion
Pluto	♇	Passion, Intensity, Regeneration

HOUSES

Just as planets move through the signs of the
zodiac, they also move through the houses in an
individual chart. The 12 houses correspond to the
12 signs, but are individualized, based upon your

sign. In this book we use Solar Houses, which place your sun sign in your 1st House. Therefore, when a planet enters a new sign it also enters a new house. If you know your exact time of birth, the rising sign determines the 1st House. You can learn your rising sign by entering your birth date at:

http://www.tarot.com/astrology/astroprofile

HOUSE	SIGN	KEYWORDS
1st House	Aries	Self, Appearance, Personality
2nd House	Taurus	Possessions, Values, Self-Worth
3rd House	Gemini	Communication, Siblings, Short Trips
4th House	Cancer	Home, Family, Roots
5th House	Leo	Love, Romance, Children, Play
6th House	Virgo	Work, Health, Daily Routines
7th House	Libra	Marriage, Relationships, Business Partners
8th House	Scorpio	Intimacy, Transformation, Shared Resources
9th House	Sagittarius	Travel, Higher Education, Philosophy
10th House	Capricorn	Career, Community, Ambition
11th House	Aquarius	Groups and Friends, Associations, Social Ideals
12th House	Pisces	Imagination, Spirituality, Secret Activities

ASPECTS

As the planets move through the sky in their various cycles, they form ever-changing angles with one another. Certain angles create significant geometric shapes. So, when two planets are 90 degrees apart, they conform to a square; 60 degrees of separation conforms to a sextile, or six-pointed star. Planets create **aspects** when they're at these special angles. Aspects explain how the individual symbolism of pairs of planets combine into an energetic pattern.

ASPECT	DEGREES	KEYWORDS
Conjunction	0	Compression, Blending, Focus
Opposition	180	Tension, Awareness, Balance
Trine	120	Harmony, Free-Flowing, Ease
Square	90	Resistance, Stress, Dynamic Conflict
Quintile	72	Creativity, Metaphysical, Magic
Sextile	60	Support, Intelligent, Activating
Quincunx	150	Irritation, Annoyance, Adjustment

2010 GENERAL FORECAST:
THE INDIVIDUAL AND THE COLLECTIVE

Astrology works for individuals, groups, and even for humanity as a whole. You will have your own story in 2010, but it will unfold among nearly seven billion other tales of human experience. We are each unique, yet our lives touch one another; our destinies are woven together by weather and war, by the economy, science, music, politics, religion, and all the other threads of life on planet Earth. We make personal choices every day, yet great events are beyond the control of anyone. When a town is flooded, it affects everyone, yet personal astrology patterns will describe the specific response of each person. Our existence is both an individual and a collective experience.

We are living in a time when the tools of self-awareness fill books, TV and radio shows, Web sites, podcasts, newspapers, and DVDs, and we benefit greatly from them. Yet despite of all this wisdom, conflicts cause enormous suffering every day. Understanding personal issues is a powerful means for increasing happiness, but knowledge of our collective issues is equally important for our safety, sanity, and well-being. This astrological look at the major trends and planetary patterns for 2010 provides a framework for comprehending the potentials and challenges we face together, so that we can advance with tolerance and respect as a community and fulfill our potential as individuals.

The astrological events used for this forecast are the transits of major planets Jupiter and Saturn, the retrograde cycles of Mercury, and the eclipses of the Sun and the Moon.

A NOTE ABOUT THE DATES IN THIS BOOK

All events are based upon the Eastern Time Zone of the United States. Because of local time differences, an event occurring just a few minutes after midnight in the East will actually happen the prior day in the rest of the country. Although the key dates are the exact dates of any particular alignment, some of you are so ready for certain things to happen that you can react to a transit a day or two before it is exact. And sometimes you can be so entrenched in habits or unwilling to change that you may not notice the effects right away. Allow extra time around each key date to feel the impact of any event.

JUPITER IN PISCES:
WILD WAVES OF CHANGE
January 17, 2010–June 6, 2010
September 9, 2010–January 22, 2011

Jupiter, the planet of expansion, reconnects us with our spiritual roots in its watery home sign of Pisces. Knowledge is no longer an intellectual abstraction; it is a living experience that comes from our connection to the cosmos. Imagination is stronger now as the limits of logic are dissolved in the boundless waters of intuition, which seem to reveal answers to all life's questions. The great gift of Jupiter in Pisces is that wisdom is equally available to everyone. The challenge, though, is connecting the grand vision that inspires us with the specific steps required to turn it into reality. Fortunately, Jupiter's foray into action-oriented Aries provides the fire to set concepts into motion.

JUPITER IN ARIES:
A GLIMPSE OF THE FUTURE
June 6, 2010–September 9, 2010
January 22, 2011–June 4, 2011

A new day dawns with farseeing Jupiter in pioneering Aries. The urge to test ideas on the battlefield of experience amplifies impatience yet rewards individuals and institutions willing to take risks. Breakthroughs in energy generation are now possible. Innovations in

education and travel are likely to follow. However,
a lack of compromise on ideological matters can
increase the potential for conflict. Bold statements and
actions provoke rapid responses, reducing the effec-
tiveness of diplomacy. Jupiter's stressful aspects with
Saturn, Uranus, and Pluto may pit progressive forces
against those who resist change. On the positive side,
new ways of seeing ourselves can quickly break down
old barriers, allowing our common humanity to overcome the differences of nationality, ideology, religion,
gender, and race.

SATURN IN VIRGO:
HEALTHY VIGILANCE
September 2, 2007–October 29, 2009
April 7, 2010–July 21, 2010

Saturn, the planet of boundaries and limitations, takes
twenty-nine years to orbit the Sun and pass through
all twelve signs of the zodiac. It demands serious
responsibility, reveals the work necessary to overcome
obstacles, and teaches us how to structure our lives.
Saturn thrives on patience and commitment, rewarding
well-planned and persistent effort while punishing
sloppiness and procrastination with disappointment,
delay, and even failure.

Saturn's passage through methodical Virgo is a
time to perfect skills, cut waste, and develop healthier
habits. Virgo is less interested in unrestrained

consumerism than in acquiring useful things. This opens the door to a new era of less conspicuous consumption and shifts the economy away from purchases of SUVs, big homes, and luxury items. Issues relating to impure food and water have already been in the news, with outbreaks of salmonella and E. coli poisoning raising wider concerns about contamination and urging us to improve our diets. Environmental concerns continue to escalate as we approach a critical point in the relationship between humanity and planet Earth. Fortunately, Saturn in exacting Virgo is also excellent for cleaning up unhealthy toxins produced by old technologies and building new ecologically friendly systems for the future.

SATURN IN LIBRA:
SURGE OF DIPLOMACY
October 29, 2009–April 7, 2010
July 21, 2010–October 5, 2012

Saturn's shift into peace-loving Libra marks a new chapter in all kinds of relationships, but there's some tough work to be done before harmony can be achieved. Saturn in Libra marks a time of significant legal changes when the scales of justice are recalibrated. The famous *Brown v. Board of Education* case—critical to reversing segregation in the United States—was launched in 1951 with Saturn in Libra. During this cycle, the legal definition of marriage is under reconsideration as we weigh and balance the spreading acceptance of same-sex marriages against the more traditional approach. The US Fairness Doctrine, which requires broadcasters to present contrasting views regarding controversial issues of public interest, could come up for scrutiny. Even challenges to international treaties governing war and peace can be expected.

When Saturn in Libra functions at its best, cooperation and civility allow diplomacy to flourish as reason replaces force. The need to weigh both sides of any argument can slow personal and public dialogue, yet it's worth the price to build bridges over seemingly impassable chasms. The negative side of Saturn, though, is its potential for rigidity, which can manifest now as a stubborn unwillingness to listen. Resistance to opposing points of view is simply an opportunity to test their worth; only with careful consideration can they be properly evaluated. Responsible individuals and wise leaders recognize the importance of treating others with respect as a foundation for any healthy relationship.

MERCURY RETROGRADES
December 26, 2009–January 15, 2010 in Capricorn / April 18–May 11 in Taurus / August 20–September 12 in Virgo / December 10 in Capricorn, Direct December 30 in Sagittarius

All true planets appear to move backward from time to time, because we view them from the moving platform of Earth. The most significant retrograde cycles are those of Mercury, the communication planet. Occurring three or four times a year for roughly three weeks at a time, these are periods when difficulties with travel, communication, details, and technical matters are likely.

Although many people think that Mercury's retrograde is negative, you can make this cycle work for you. Because personal and commercial interactions are emphasized, you can actually accomplish more than usual, especially if you stay focused on what needs to be done rather than initiating new projects. Still, you may feel as if you're treading water—or worse, carried backward in an undertow of unfinished business. Worry less about making progress than about the quality of your work. Pay extra attention to all your communication exchanges. Avoiding misunderstandings and omissions is the ideal way to minimize complications. Retrograde Mercury is best used to tie up loose ends as you review, redo, reconsider, and, in general, revisit the past.

This year, all four retrogrades begin in practical earth signs (Capricorn, Taurus, Virgo), challenging us to redefine our material values, ambitions, and methods. Sticking to literal interpretations of reality during these periods can be extremely limiting. We are pushed to question our perceptions and break the forms of recognition and description that bind us to our current ways of seeing and communicating. Intuitive approaches in which the subjective qualities of life take on more importance fill in the gaps where objective analyses fall short.

ECLIPSES
Solar: January 15 and July 11
Lunar: June 26 and December 21

Solar and Lunar Eclipses are special New and Full
Moons that indicate significant changes for individuals
and groups. They are powerful markers of events with
influences that can appear up to three months in
advance and last up to six months afterward.

January 15, Solar Eclipse in Capricorn:
Fall from Grace

The powerful changes of this eclipse are softened by its close conjunction with gentle Venus. Heads of state—especially female—may fall, but they're likely to land in cushy places with the planet of love and rewards in the picture. A supportive sextile from inventive Uranus encourages alternative forms of leadership and helpful shakeups in large organizations. This eclipse is visible through the middle of China, the southern tip of India, and Central Africa, making its impact stronger in these areas.

June 26, Lunar Eclipse in Capricorn:
Sudden Exposure

This Lunar Eclipse is conjunct insatiable Pluto, indicating major issues that threaten safety and security. Abuse of power is likely, especially in traditional institutions that have long resisted reform and exposure to public scrutiny. Toxicity can be a concern with Pluto's presence, perhaps affecting food supplies. The volatile conjunction of Jupiter and Uranus square the eclipse may precipitate rapid changes that unexpectedly undermine the viability of influential organizations. Positively, a healthy purge can restore life to fading companies and failing governments.

July 11, Solar Eclipse in Cancer:
Water Works
The potential for problems is considerable with this
Total Eclipse of the Sun conjunct the karmic South
Node of the Moon. Water may be threatened by pollution
or become threatening itself through storms and flood-
ing. Fortunately, Mars in efficient Virgo forms an intelligent sextile to the eclipse that provides rapid responses
whenever corrective action is needed. The vast majority
of the path of visibility falls over water in the South
Pacific, reducing its area of influence. It does touch the
southern tip of South America, where its effects may be
more evident.

December 21, Lunar Eclipse in Gemini:
Static on the Line
Tranquility on the home front and travel for the holidays
may be disturbed by this Total Lunar Eclipse in the
chatty transportation sign of Gemini. Intense Pluto and
talkative Mercury oppose the Moon, triggering provoca-
tive conversations and communication breakdowns. The
Jupiter-Uranus conjunction squares the eclipse, adding
another degree of instability that could trigger earth-
quakes or unusual weather. Still, brilliant ideas can
explode from unexpected sources to drastically shift
our perceptions and the ways in which we connect with
one another.

THE BOTTOM LINE:
SAVE THE HUMANS

All the talk about transformational shifts in 2010 at the
supposed end of the Mayan calendar overlooks the
incredible planetary forces that will reshape the future
of humanity this year. Undoubtedly there will be major
changes during slow-moving Uranus-Pluto squares of
2012–2015, reawakening the energy of the mid-1960s
when revolutionary Uranus conjoined evolutionary
Pluto. But we don't need to wait until then—when it
may be too late—to start the work that so desperately
needs to be done. The formative forces of the outer
planets aligning at the beginning of the cardinal signs
in 2010 suggest that the new era is opening now. The
movements of expansive Jupiter and structuring Saturn
from season-ending mutable signs where old energy is
released to the initiating signs of Aries and Libra are
enough by themselves to tell the tale of an emerging
new world order.

Our least viable option, and most unlikely scenario, is
standing still in a futile attempt to maintain the status
quo. The year 2010 is not one of stagnation; it's a year
when the slow simmer of unresolved issues boils over
and demands our attention. The degree of stress is
high, yet the potential for finally making the structural
changes and sacrifices necessary to save humanity
does exist. This is, happily, not some dreary trudge
toward inevitable failure, but a turning point when the

pressure of physical stress crosses with the genius
of human potential to take us on a healthier and more
hopeful path to the future.

Remember that all these astrological events are
part of the general cosmic weather of the year, but will
affect us each differently based on our individual
astrological signs.

LIBRA
AUGUST–DECEMBER
2009 OVERVIEW

RIDING THE SEESAW OF LIFE

Your struggle to gain control of certain aspects of your life may be a recurring theme this month, beginning on **August 1** as Venus, the Goddess of Love, engages in a standoff with potent Pluto. The month ends with Mars, the God of War, entangled in the same tug-of-war on **August 26**. Between this challenging pair of dramatic oppositions, you may attempt to carve out a balance between opportunities to enjoy yourself and your responsibilities to finish what you've already started. The Full Moon Eclipse in nonconformist Aquarius on **August 5** falls in your creative 5th House, suggesting a breakthrough in how you express yourself. If you're involved with any type of artistic endeavor, this is the time for a radical approach—you may discover exciting ways to advance your technique. The 5th House is also associated with children, so you could have a surprising interaction with a clever child who teaches you something you might not expect from a youngster.

Overconfident Jupiter in your 5th House of Love and Play forms an aggravating quincunx with serious Saturn in your 12th House of Endings on **August 19**—the second of three such aspects that began on **March 22** and culminates on **February 5, 2010**. You may be quite clear about what you want and what you need to do, yet executing your plan won't necessarily set things right. For now, accept the presence of unresolvable extremes in your life, even as you strive for more moderation. The fixed Leo New Moon on **August 20** falls in your 11th House of Goals, indicating your unwillingness to simply go with the flow. You have an agenda and are determined to stick to it, even if progress is temporarily elusive.

SATURDAY 1 ★ Don't miss an opportunity to discuss your feelings

SUNDAY 2 ★

MONDAY 3 ★

TUESDAY 4 ★

WEDNESDAY 5 ★ ○

THURSDAY 6

FRIDAY 7

SATURDAY 8

SUNDAY 9

MONDAY 10 ★ You overcome obstacles and see your confidence return

TUESDAY 11 ★

WEDNESDAY 12 ★

THURSDAY 13 ★

FRIDAY 14 ★

SATURDAY 15

SUNDAY 16

MONDAY 17 ★ **SUPER NOVA DAYS** Clear the air with a heartfelt expression of your feelings

TUESDAY 18 ★

WEDNESDAY 19 ★

THURSDAY 20 ★ ●

FRIDAY 21

SATURDAY 22

SUNDAY 23

MONDAY 24

TUESDAY 25 ★ Patience is the smarter strategy

WEDNESDAY 26 ★

THURSDAY 27

FRIDAY 28

SATURDAY 29

SUNDAY 30

MONDAY 31

★ designates key date

DESTINY CALLS

If you have trouble making decisions, it's because you so often see both sides of an issue better than other people do. This month finds you pressed to choose between taking a risk and following a more conventional path. Ultimately, this is a turning point, even if you're uncertain about your current choices. No matter what you do, you're nearing the end of a long-term cycle on **September 12** when karmic Saturn in your 12th House of Endings opposes radical Uranus. Remember the fork in the road you faced at the previous Saturn-Uranus oppositions on **November 4, 2008**, and **February 5** as you manage this transition. The conflict between holding on to your past and stepping into your future is significant enough that it will require additional time to resolve. The final recurrence of this stressful aspect is on **July 26, 2010**, yet the immediate sense of urgency is still great. Saturn's imbalanced quincunx to foggy Neptune on **September 12** further muddies what's happening, for Neptune's influence from your 5th House of Love and Play may deceive you into believing you can avoid serious issues. Additionally, Mercury the Messenger is in its trickster phase—retrograde from **September 4 to September 29**—urging you to revisit and revise previously made plans.

The psychic Pisces Full Moon on **September 4** falls in your 6th House of Details, overloading you with more than you care to handle. The efficient Virgo New Moon on **September 18**, however, is conjunct unyielding Saturn, focusing your attention on the crucial issues and empowering you to push through these major changes.

TUESDAY 1	
WEDNESDAY 2	
THURSDAY 3 ★	All forms of communication take center stage now
FRIDAY 4 ★ ○	
SATURDAY 5	
SUNDAY 6	
MONDAY 7	
TUESDAY 8	
WEDNESDAY 9	
THURSDAY 10	
FRIDAY 11 ★	Avoidance isn't a viable long-term strategy
SATURDAY 12 ★	
SUNDAY 13	
MONDAY 14	
TUESDAY 15 ★	**SUPER NOVA DAYS** Discern fact from fiction in order to move on
WEDNESDAY 16 ★	
THURSDAY 17 ★	
FRIDAY 18 ★ ●	
SATURDAY 19	
SUNDAY 20 ★	Simplify your relationships and eliminate distractions
MONDAY 21	
TUESDAY 22 ★	Dramatic breakthroughs are possible
WEDNESDAY 23 ★	
THURSDAY 24	
FRIDAY 25	
SATURDAY 26	
SUNDAY 27	
MONDAY 28	
TUESDAY 29	
WEDNESDAY 30	

BEFORE THE HARVEST

You're reaching the culmination of a two-year process clearing away psychic undergrowth from your subconscious mind. Expect challenges as you work to complete old business before serious Saturn leaves your 12th House of Soul Consciousness on **October 29**. It's difficult now to see what fruits your labor will bear over the next couple of years when Saturn the Tester moves through Libra. In any case, your efforts are better aimed at tying up loose ends while there's still time. Instead of focusing on any failures, remember that pruning back your tree of life will encourage healthier growth ahead.

The self-centered Aries New Moon on **October 4** falls in your 7th House of Partnerships, placing you in the middle of a passionate tug-of-war. On the one hand, you recognize what others want and are drawn to providing it, if you can. On the other, you may feel that it's high time you satisfied your own needs, rather than always being the gracious one who acquiesces to make everyone else happy. Luckily, you can juggle your personal yearnings with your thirst for pleasing others as the Sun moves through relationship-oriented Libra until **October 23**. You receive additional assistance from thoughtful Mercury as it enters diplomatic Libra on **October 9**, followed by your ruling planet, Venus, on **October 14**. You are very much at home playing on both sides of the fence now. The reflective Libra New Moon on **October 18** harmonizes with spiritual Neptune, blessing you with grace, adding inspiration to your artful pursuits, and gently reminding you to believe in your dreams.

THURSDAY 1

FRIDAY 2

SATURDAY 3

SUNDAY 4 ★ ○ Let everyone know where you stand

MONDAY 5

TUESDAY 6

WEDNESDAY 7

THURSDAY 8 ★ Analyze and process your deepest feelings

FRIDAY 9 ★

SATURDAY 10 ★

SUNDAY 11

MONDAY 12 ★ SUPER NOVA DAYS Be more patient before seeking any tangible rewards

TUESDAY 13 ★

WEDNESDAY 14 ★

THURSDAY 15 ★

FRIDAY 16

SATURDAY 17

SUNDAY 18 ●

MONDAY 19

TUESDAY 20

WEDNESDAY 21

THURSDAY 22

FRIDAY 23 ★ Your emotions pick up additional intensity

SATURDAY 24 ★

SUNDAY 25

MONDAY 26

TUESDAY 27

WEDNESDAY 28 ★ Learn an important lesson about appreciating pleasure

THURSDAY 29 ★

FRIDAY 30

SATURDAY 31

DECONSTRUCTION ZONE

There's no room for laziness now that hardworking Saturn is in your sign, but rest assured that your extra efforts will be recognized and rewarded, even if it takes time. Having Saturn in your 1st House of Self for the next couple of years may mean significant adjustments, but the sooner you realize that this is serious business, the easier life will be. Saturn forms a dynamic square with transformative Pluto on **November 15**—the first of three such transitions that recur on **January 31, 2010**, and **August 21, 2010**. The stressful connection between these two tough planetary heavyweights can exhaust you, so manage your time and resources carefully. You may win battle after battle yet still lose the war if you're overconfident or in denial. Pluto is in your 4th House of Roots, indicating that the metamorphosis will affect the most stable and fundamental areas of your life, including your home and family. Nevertheless, this intense process continues through the rest of the year, leaving you stronger and wiser if you're up for the challenge.

The stubborn Taurus Full Moon on **November 2** falls in your 8th House of Investments and Shared Resources, tempting you to hold on to what you've already earned. Trust feelings over logical analysis and don't get bogged down with too many facts, for they could actually mislead you now. Then, on **November 16**, a complex Scorpio New Moon occurs in your 2nd House of Personal Resources. Like the earlier Full Moon, this one can be hard on your pocketbook unless you pay close attention. Even if financial pressure subsides toward the end of the month, don't let up on your due diligence and determination.

SUNDAY 1

MONDAY 2 ★ ○ An easygoing manner makes you likable

TUESDAY 3

WEDNESDAY 4

THURSDAY 5

FRIDAY 6

SATURDAY 7 ★ Raise the bar of excellence on intimacy

SUNDAY 8 ★

MONDAY 9 ★

TUESDAY 10 ★

WEDNESDAY 11

THURSDAY 12

FRIDAY 13

SATURDAY 14 ★ **SUPER NOVA DAYS** Dare yourself to break free from your routine

SUNDAY 15 ★

MONDAY 16 ★ ●

TUESDAY 17

WEDNESDAY 18

THURSDAY 19

FRIDAY 20

SATURDAY 21

SUNDAY 22

MONDAY 23 ★ Go ahead and treat yourself to a well-deserved vacation

TUESDAY 24 ★

WEDNESDAY 25 ★

THURSDAY 26 ★

FRIDAY 27

SATURDAY 28

SUNDAY 29

MONDAY 30

BEAUTIFUL DREAMER

A rainbow that vanished in a recent storm may reappear this month, tempting you to look again for the legendary pot of gold as benevolent Jupiter conjuncts healing Chiron on **December 7** and mystical Neptune on **December 21**. These idealistic conjunctions are the culmination of an ongoing pattern that began in May and July, and that continues to open your heart and mind to your own creativity. Now, as this magical super-conjunction coalesces for the third and final time, you mustn't miss the opportunity to actualize your dreams. Paradoxically, you cannot be greedy—if you try to grab too much, it will all just disappear like a mirage. Balance reality with your hopes as best you can. Fortunately, you receive cosmic assistance that enables you to keep your feet on the ground as messenger Mercury enters traditional Capricorn on **December 5**, followed by the willful Sun on **December 21** and sensual Venus on **December 25**. Be prepared to journey into the transformative shadows of change as each of these planets conjuncts dark Pluto—already in Capricorn—on **December 7, December 24, and December 28**.

Your confidence increases, and you might believe that your success is near on **December 16** as the enthusiastic Sagittarius New Moon supports the inspirational trio of Jupiter, Chiron, and Neptune. But everything may take longer than you wish, because action-hero Mars slows down and turns retrograde on **December 20**, followed by communicator Mercury's backward turn on **December 26**. You may feel weary or even defeated, but don't give up; you just need some time to relax. Your ambition will get a second wind after the self-protective Cancer Full Moon Eclipse clears the air on **December 31**.

TUESDAY 1 ★ Find satisfaction right where you are

WEDNESDAY 2 ★ ○

THURSDAY 3

FRIDAY 4

SATURDAY 5

SUNDAY 6

MONDAY 7 ★ Be relentless in your pursuit of happiness

TUESDAY 8

WEDNESDAY 9

THURSDAY 10

FRIDAY 11

SATURDAY 12

SUNDAY 13

MONDAY 14 ★ **SUPER NOVA DAYS** Step outside the box to reach your goals

TUESDAY 15 ★

WEDNESDAY 16 ★ ●

THURSDAY 17 ★

FRIDAY 18

SATURDAY 19 ★ Your dreams are alive and harmonized with the idealistic

SUNDAY 20 ★

MONDAY 21 ★

TUESDAY 22

WEDNESDAY 23

THURSDAY 24

FRIDAY 25

SATURDAY 26

SUNDAY 27

MONDAY 28 ★ Intense emotions now suggest that the New Year will be anything but boring

TUESDAY 29 ★

WEDNESDAY 30 ★

THURSDAY 31 ★ ○

2010 HOROSCOPE

LIBRA

SEPTEMBER 23–OCTOBER 22

OVERVIEW OF THE YEAR

Although you naturally excel at creating harmony where there is discord, your skills of diplomacy will be severely tested this year. First and foremost, Saturn the Taskmaster entered your sign on October 29, 2009, for a visit that lasts until October 5, 2012. You are already in the process of finishing old business to prepare for new opportunities ahead. But Saturn's journey through your 1st House of Self may feel like a burden that can stress the very foundations of your life. If you're on the right track and have been doing solid work, Saturn will bring you the rewards you've earned. However, judgmental Saturn will also demonstrate where you have failed or areas of your life that now need critical attention. It's crucial to view any current difficulties you now face as messages from the stern planet. **Don't waste time and energy feeling sorry for yourself; overcome your weariness or depression by executing a workable plan to meet the challenges.** But don't expect a simple pass-or-fail grade on Saturn's report card, for you're more likely to find success in some quarters of your life and disappointment in others.

Don't be surprised if you can't move forward as fast as you want, for Saturn will slow you down until you get it right. When Saturn retrogrades back into analytical Virgo and your 12th House of Endings on April 7—where it was for the previous two years—you will be required to tie up loose ends to lighten your load. **This is no time for laziness;** it will be much easier to settle karmic debts before Saturn reenters your sign on July 21.

Transformative Pluto adds intensity while stirring up issues from your past as it moves through your 4th House of Roots. **You're convinced you just don't have the time or resources to get ahead of the waves of change.** Saturn's square to unrelenting Pluto began on November 15, 2009, to remind you that you cannot do it all. This suppressive aspect recurs on January 31 and August 21, demanding that you cut back inessential activities and eliminate unhealthy relationships. Additionally, rebellious Uranus continues its long standoff with traditional Saturn, forcing you to break free of tension by taking radical action, especially around April 26 and July 26.

Fortunately, **there is also excitement on your horizon** as **Uranus the Awakener opens your eyes to new relationship possibilities**, especially when it visits enthusiastic Aries and your 7th House of Partnerships from May 27 through August 13. Although the planet spends the rest of the year disrupting your day-to-day activities, it's a familiar pattern—Uranus has been in your 6th House of Daily Routines since 2003. Opportunistic Jupiter joins the Awakener on June 8 and September 18 to blast you out of complacency and into your future. Their third and final conjunction doesn't occur until January 4, 2011, yet your anticipation of change will build throughout the end of the year.

SOMEWHERE OVER THE RAINBOW

Your hopes are high as the year begins. Optimistic Jupiter and poetic Neptune are in your 5th House of Love, but dreamy potential bumps into practical logistics as Jupiter enters your 6th House of Habits on January 17. Still, you aren't ready to give up your ideals, for sweet Venus is in your romantic 5th House from January 18 to February 11, reinforced by communicator Mercury from February 10 to March 1. Valentine's Day magic is fed by its proximity to a beautiful Venus-Jupiter conjunction on February 16, making this an opportune time to express your heart's desire. The Jupiter-Uranus conjunction on June 8 falls in your 7th House of Relationships, giving you a glimpse of a perfect yet unconventional partnership. But before you can fulfill your dreams, you must overcome your own sense of limitations: Restrictive Saturn opposes independent Uranus on April 26 and July 26 and excessive Jupiter on May 23 and August 16.

IT TAKES TWO

So much of your career success depends on the quality of your work relationships. As a Libra, you need others to reach your highest potential, yet this year your partners can serve up shocking surprises as generous Jupiter joins unpredictable Uranus in your 7th House of Others on June 8. Although a business associate could easily promise you the world, delivery may be a bit more difficult. With reliable Saturn opposing Jupiter and Uranus through the spring and summer, caution is advised; do your homework in advance to minimize the effects of someone else's erratic behavior. A Solar Eclipse in your 10th House of Career on July 11 is supported by action-planet Mars, so use this time to act on your dreams in ways that help you reach your goals the rest of the year.

SLOW GROWTH

Be careful about pursuing opportunities with someone who confidently paints a picture of success, especially when Jupiter is in your 7th House of Partners from June 6 to September 9. With austere Saturn in Libra for most of the year, investments will take longer to reach fruition. Powerful Pluto rules your 2nd House of Money; its squares to Saturn on January 31 and August 21 are further indications of the fierce concentration and focus you'll need to achieve your financial goals. You may be short on cash when luxurious Venus is retrograde in your 2nd House of Income from October 8 to November 18. Finances should improve when she reenters your 2nd House on November 29.

A NEW YOU

You can make significant health breakthroughs this year, especially when Chiron the Healer is in intuitive Pisces and your 6th House of Health and Habits from April 20 to July 20. Indeed, you may face difficult consequences if you don't make healthy improvements to your diet, exercise program, and lifestyle, especially when Jupiter is in your 6th House from January 17 to June 6 and again from September 9 to January 22, 2011. Benevolent Jupiter joins tension-releasing Uranus in your 6th House on September 18 and January 4, 2011, extending the positive impact of this alignment into next year.

ALL IN THE FAMILY

Although evolutionary Pluto is in your 4th House of Home and Family for many years to come, the intensity it brings to this area of your life is magnified now by two eclipses. The Capricorn New Moon Eclipse on January 15 joins your key planet, Venus, in your 4th House, indicating that your home should be filled with love and beauty. But good feelings don't just happen; you must work at creating an environment in which everyone feels comfortable and respected. The Capricorn Full Moon Eclipse on June 26 is conjunct Pluto, suggesting that inevitable changes will force you to let go as someone close to you expresses a need for independence. With communicator Mercury and optimistic Jupiter in the picture, a positive outcome is likely if you're able to talk about what you want while keeping an open mind about the needs of others.

BUSINESS AND PLEASURE

You may find yourself on the road or back in school this year. Jupiter—the planet of travel and education—is in your 6th House of Work on January 17 to June 6 and again on September 9 to January 22, 2011. You're tempted to schedule a trip around the conjunction of interactive Mercury and Jupiter on March 7, yet strict Saturn could make you work hard for little in return. The emphasis shifts when Jupiter is in your 7th House of Companions from June 6 to September 9. A vacation might be in order, especially if you have a traveling partner. Even if you decide to go away for a personal retreat or a weekend workshop, it will still be more fun if you share it with some-one special.

SHIFT HAPPENS

You have much to learn about the inner workings of your mind this year, and the opportunities for spiritual growth are enormous. Disciplined Saturn first entered virtuous Virgo and your 12th House of Soul Consciousness in fall 2008. Now, as it retrogrades back there April 7–July 21, it's time to finish up your metaphysical studies and apply your knowledge to your everyday life. There is great potential for a breakthrough around June 8, when visionary Jupiter conjuncts revolutionary Uranus in your 7th House of Others. Being ready to accept the teachings of someone wise can speed your process of awakening.

RICK & JEFF'S TIP FOR THE YEAR
Rise to the Challenge

Although relationships can offer you a newfound sense of freedom this year, they can also distract you from the discipline you need to organize your life. The decisions you must make this year are not easy ones. You may have to be ruthless when evaluating what and who should be cut out of your life, but pruning is absolutely required to ensure maximum growth. Your overall success during the coming years will be based on your ability to pay careful attention to your long-term goals rather than short-term successes.

JANUARY

BOUND TO HAPPEN

You must take more responsibility for your life now as you react to the pressures of change at work and at home. With Saturn the Tester in your sign until **April 7**, your freedom of movement is restrained, allowing you to concentrate on matters of critical importance. But four planets in serious Capricorn and your 4th House of Foundations require you to look inward to your feelings and backward to your past so you can decide how to move forward into the future. Saturn's heavy square to transformational Pluto suggests that resistance is futile. You can't prevent family matters from evolving any more than you can stop the tides from shifting.

Events that began to unfold at the first Saturn-Pluto square around **November 15, 2009**, will reach a turning point on **January 31**, but won't be completely over until the third occurrence on **August 21**. You may expend a lot of energy fighting against something you don't want to happen. Your struggle will be even harder, though, if you stubbornly try to keep everything as it is.

It may be nearly impossible to make progress toward your long-term goals with energetic Mars now retrograde in your 11th House of Dreams and Wishes. You may feel stuck, both mentally and physically, because Mercury in cautious Capricorn is also retrograde until **January 15**, the same day as a Capricorn New Moon Eclipse. Mercury conjoins Pluto during this Solar Eclipse in your 4th House, catalyzing family dynamics and also driving your thoughts deeper and darker, which could result in the loosening of the ties that bind. The demonstrative Leo Full Moon on **January 30** conjuncts action-packed Mars in your 11th House, pushing you to share plans with your friends, even if you're not ready to make your move.

KEEP IN MIND THIS MONTH

Your easygoing demeanor is tested by circumstances beyond your control. Don't try to fight back on every front; instead, choose your battles carefully.

KEY DATES

★ **JANUARY 1–2**
hall of mirrors
It's hard to combine the magic of your dreams with the circumstances of your current situation. Although the Sun's creative quintile to electrifying Uranus on **January 1** increases your charisma and charm, it may be hard to tell where your fantasies end and the real world begins. Sweet Venus aligns with illusory Neptune on **January 2**, allowing you to see things as you wish them to be, not how they actually are.

★ **JANUARY 7–11**
follow your heart
The ego-driven Sun and desire-motivated Venus run into angry Mars on **January 7–8**, creating unnecessary conflict and unkindness. Your key planet, Venus, is the Sun's traveling companion now as they move toward exact conjunction on **January 11** to bring your desires and your convictions into sharp focus. Don't be afraid to trust your feelings as you reach for creative solutions outside of the box.

★ **JANUARY 13–15**
change strikes

You may be approaching the end of your rope with boredom, prompting you to take a chance when the brilliant Sun and Venus form a supportive sextile with reactionary Uranus on **January 13**. Your uncharacteristic impatience is further stirred by Mercury's direct turn and shocking Uranus's connection to the electric Solar Eclipse on **January 15**. Although you can now set significant changes into motion, it's likely to take you a few weeks to understand the potential impact of these few days.

★ **JANUARY 22**
labor of love

Venus is in your 5th House of Fun and Games, but don't expect spontaneous fireworks or playful infatuations when the planet of romance harmoniously trines mature Saturn. Instead of immediate gratification, you're concerned with sustaining a more concrete expression of love. Instead of foolishly spending your money or expressing fleeting emotions, concentrate your attention on achieving long-term satisfaction through self-restraint and persistence. This is an excellent time to sign a business deal or enter into an agreement with an intimate partner.

SUPER NOVA DAYS

★ **JANUARY 27–31**
make love, not war
The cosmic lovers, sensual Venus and passionate Mars, stand in opposition on **January 27**, activating your 5th and 11th Houses of Love. Even if you know what you want, it may be impractical to get it: Your individual needs clash with those around you. Tensions build when the Sun opposes Mars on **January 29**, followed by the self-centered Leo Full Moon conjuncting Mars on **January 30**. Seeking common ground is surely better than open combat, yet the unforgiving Saturn-Pluto square on **January 31** suggests that a real solution won't come quickly.

FEBRUARY

DREAM THE IMPOSSIBLE DREAM

You may feel as if you've been knocked off course and it's time to put your life back on track. Even if you've faced disappointment or defeat, you're being offered a chance now to create new dreams to feed your soul. You might be tempted to scale back your expectations based on your recent experiences, but downsizing would be a mistake. With buoyant Jupiter in imaginative Pisces, you can improve your daily life by practicing "wish craft," so don't be afraid to dream big! Luckily, you receive a cosmic assist from a rare conjunction between healing Chiron and inspirational Neptune on **February 17** that falls in your 5th House of Love and Creativity. Although this fantastic slow-moving alignment can nourish your spirit all month, give yourself extra playtime to explore and express your inner child when your ruling planet, Venus, conjuncts Chiron and Neptune on **February 7–8**.

The futuristic Aquarius New Moon on **February 13** activates your romantic 5th House and conjuncts both Chiron and Neptune, reinforcing your connection to your spirituality and magnifying the healing power of compassion and love. Communication will likely be animated as intelligent Mercury debates punchy Mars in a tense opposition. The Sun's conjunction to the ethereal Chiron-Neptune conjunction on **February 14** can surely light up romance on Valentine's Day, especially if you're willing to let your fantasies fuel the fun. The Full Moon in discerning Virgo on **February 28** is a conundrum, for it opposes a limitless Sun-Jupiter conjunction in mystical Pisces. Relying on critical thinking can only take you so far. Set logic aside and let your uninhibited intuition reveal what's in your future.

KEEP IN MIND THIS MONTH

Don't be afraid to trust your dreams, even if the possibilities before you appear limited. Your horizons will continue to broaden as long as you keep hope alive.

KEY DATES

★ **FEBRUARY 2**
love hurts

You may feel isolated when loving Venus in
your 5th House of Romance and Self-
Expression runs into resistance from heavyweights Saturn and Pluto. It's time to address
powerful emotions in your relationships. Yes,
it's hard work that you may prefer to avoid, but
the results can be profound, even if there are
no simple answers. Fortunately, the energy
will lighten up in a day or two.

★ **FEBRUARY 5–8**
no holds barred

It's challenging not to take things very personally now. Try to look at any dissatisfaction over
achieving your goals in a larger context on
February 5, when cheerful Jupiter forms an
irritating quincunx to realistic Saturn. Luckily,
Jupiter's uplifting vision is strengthened the
next day by passionate Pluto. You can reach
deeply within to drive yourself toward your
dreams. Sweet Venus joins maverick Chiron

on **February 7** and dream-weaving Neptune on
February 8, encouraging you to aspire toward
a more fulfilling future. Give yourself permission
to want more than you have without guilt.

★ **FEBRUARY 10–13**
dancing in the dark
On **February 10–12**, retrograde Mars compli-
cates your social life as it forms frustrating
quincunxes with lavish Jupiter and shadowy
Pluto. A friend or associate could easily misinterpret your impulsive actions now. Trickster
Mercury is quick on the draw as it enters
progressive Aquarius on **February 10** and
fortunately harmonizes with sobering Saturn
on **February 12** to slow you down. If you're
not sure what to do, then don't do anything
at all until after the Aquarius New Moon
on **February 13**.

SUPER NOVA DAYS

★ **FEBRUARY 16–18**
imagine
Everything seems to fit into place on the job
when lovely Venus conjuncts prosperous

Jupiter in your 6th House of Employment on **February 16**. It's hard to avoid falling in love, even if it's only with an illusion. The imaginative Chiron-Neptune conjunction on **February 17** pushes back the edges of reality and could have you chasing after the pot of gold at the end of every rainbow you can find. The Sun's entry into mythical Pisces on **February 18** is just one more reminder of how important your spiritual life is these days.

★ **FEBRUARY 28**
just say yes
The month ends on a very positive note as the Sun's annual conjunction with abundant Jupiter punctuates the soulful 12th House Virgo Full Moon with exclamation points of peace, love, and understanding. Although your desire to remain objective may hold you back, opportunity seems to be knocking; you'd be wise to open the door and let it in. Nevertheless, there's nothing wrong with using your common sense and maintaining a bit of pragmatic caution.

MARCH

GET BUSY

Taking care of business has you on the move when this month begins with five planets in your 6th House of Work and Hobbies. It's a smart idea to stick to a schedule or you might just run around in circles without accomplishing much. The emphasis on work starts to diminish when your ruling planet, Venus, leaves the detail-oriented 6th House to enter headstrong Aries and your 7th House of Relationships on **March 7**. Loving Venus takes you on an emotional roller-coaster ride **March 7–11** when she is excited by a trine to Mars, stopped in her tracks by an opposition to stern Saturn, and pulled into dark shadows by intense Pluto. On **March 10**—in the midst of this planetary shuffle—Mars, in your 11th House of Goals, ends a retrograde period that began on **December 20, 2009**. It may take a few days to really feel the difference, but you should soon be able to tell that your life is finally moving forward again.

The psychic Pisces New Moon on **March 15** is a wake-up call that can unveil a totally different way to get your work done. Trying something new

can lead to a significant breakthrough. Your interactions with others continue to deepen when
Mercury enters your 7th House of Companions
on **March 17**, followed there by the Sun on
March 20, the Spring Equinox. Although you
prefer to sidestep conflict, the socially adept
Libra Full Moon on **March 29** can also skillfully
bring tension out into the open. This is an opportune time to engage in discussions that can
restore lost harmony to any personal or business
relationship in distress.

KEEP IN MIND THIS MONTH

*Don't gauge your happiness on how someone else is
feeling. The best way to maintain a healthy balance
in relationships is to first take care of yourself.*

KEY DATES

★ **MARCH 3-4**
building a mystery
Turning your world topsy-turvy sounds like fun when sweet Venus joins rowdy Uranus in your 6th House of Daily Routines on **March 3**. You aren't constrained by the usual rules now, so you could make choices that seem out of character. Fortunately, communicator Mercury receives support from potent Pluto on **March 4**, infusing your words with passion. But immediate gratification won't bring lasting satisfaction unless you delve into the emotional wetlands and touch what's hiding in the dark of your subconscious mind.

SUPER NOVA DAYS

★ **MARCH 7-11**
many faces of love
Charming Venus rushes into courageous Aries, teaching you how to be more assertive about what you want from a partner. Venus's trine to physical Mars on **March 7** is good news that portends the uncomplicated kind of

73

interactions you like—and talkative Mercury's conjunction to extroverted Jupiter that same day enhances your gift of gab. Be careful what you ask for because you just might get it. The sweet message of love changes when Venus's tense opposition to showstopping Saturn on **March 9** slams the brakes on your pleasant journey. You are uncharacteristically driven to go after what you want when Venus's dynamic square to obsessive Pluto on **March 11** intensifies your desires. Even if you're sure this is a win-or-lose situation, the severity will ease over the days ahead.

★ **MARCH 15**
fresh start
Your nervous system is overstimulated and crackling with electricity as the hypersensitive Pisces New Moon conjuncts jumpy Mercury and shaky Uranus. This New Moon falls in your 6th House of Health and Habits, giving you a new perspective on how unhealthy lifestyle patterns could negatively impact your well-being. Luckily, positive thinking can spark the lightning of awareness to clear out the

tangled underbrush of outdated habitual
thoughts. Plant seeds of intention now, for
you can successfully turn a good idea into
daily practice.

★ **MARCH 17–22**
all together now
The days surrounding the Spring Equinox
on **March 20** buzz with excitement. New
people enter your life to ignite your enthusiasm and propel you forward as Mercury the
Communicator blasts into incorrigible Aries on
March 17 and your 7th House of Companions.
The Sun's annual conjunction with alarming
Uranus on the same day can startle you
awake, yet its opposition to restrictive Saturn
on **March 21** prevents you from squandering
your energy in an impulsive outburst that's all
noise with little lasting value. A fortunate
Mars-Saturn sextile on **March 22** assures that
your hard work is worth it, as long as you
involve others in your plan, pace yourself, and
pay attention to the details.

APRIL

WHEN PUSH COMES TO SHOVE

Saturn the Taskmaster has required you to take greater responsibility for your life ever since it entered your sign on **October 29, 2009**. On **April 7**, it retrogrades back into detail-oriented Virgo and your 12th House of Endings, offering you one more chance to break out of unhealthy patterns that no longer serve you. The tension between respecting tradition and rebelling against it increases throughout the month; you're finally forced to do something about it when stern Saturn opposes wayward Uranus on **April 26**. This is part of a long-term transition that began on **November 4, 2008**, and culminates on **July 26**— one that can revitalize your relationships and have you challenging authority in order to bring about necessary change.

The self-starting Aries New Moon on **April 14** falls in your 7th House of Partners, an opportune time to review your needs in relation to others. Finding a healthy balance between individual goals and mutual dreams can be tricky, yet Mercury and Venus are both in your 8th House of Intimacy and Transformation, allowing you to talk it out. Additionally, Mercury's retrograde period from **April 18 to May 11** is a time to reconsider old assumptions, share them with someone you trust, and perhaps consult a therapist. You can get a lot of mileage from psychological and spiritual tools now if you apply them to deepening your connection with others rather than justifying your retreat. On **April 28**, the passionate Scorpio Full Moon in your 2nd House of Self-Worth opposes Mercury in determined Taurus, giving you the strength to hold your ground when negotiating with others. However, you may need to scale back your demands, for the Full Moon's square to feisty Mars can make you uncharacteristically combative.

KEEP IN MIND THIS MONTH

The need to shake up your life can provoke rash actions. Remember, there's no need to rush; changes will continue to happen.

KEY DATES

★ **APRIL 3–6**
a pair of hearts
Clever Mercury and creative Venus are traveling companions now in your 8th House of Deep Sharing, motivating you to take conversations about love into vulnerable places in search of additional meaning. Together, they square contentious Mars in dramatic Leo, bringing you to the edge of verbal combat. You know what you want, you express it, and you're willing to show that you mean it. Fortunately, Mercury and Venus also create agreeable trines with evolutionary Pluto, allowing you to magically transform a potential conflict into an intimate moment if you're willing to join someone in unknown emotional territory.

★ **APRIL 10**
claiming your space
Even if you're sure a recent power struggle is over, another layer of emotional dissonance becomes apparent when aggressive Mars attempts to exert control over domineering

Pluto. Well-meaning friends could be the source of annoyance now as Mars in your 11th House of Teamwork forms an irritating quincunx with Pluto in your 4th House of Security. If others are intruding into your personal business without your permission, you'll need to set boundaries even if it means an unpleasant skirmish. A magical Mercury-Neptune quintile, though, could give you exactly the right words to smooth ruffled feathers without surrendering any territory.

★ APRIL 17–18
separation anxiety
Your desires deepen on **April 17** thanks to the influence of fervent Pluto. Total satisfaction may be elusive, yet sensual Venus receives support from hopeful Jupiter to bring you a temporary peace offering. But intellectual Mercury turns retrograde in your 8th House of Shared Resources on **April 18**, slowing communications and increasing the distance between you and a partner. Don't waste energy fighting this mental undertow. Instead, learn what you can by revisiting recent love lessons

so that you can apply them when the
opportunity returns.

SUPER NOVA DAYS

★ **APRIL 22–26**
fasten your seat belt
Romantic Venus forms a creative quintile to
physical Mars on **April 22** and a problematic
square to illusory Neptune on **April 23**, tempting you with the magic of love that could leave
you with an unrealizable fantasy. Then Venus
connects with runaway Uranus on the **23rd**
and restrained Saturn on the **24th**, offering you
freedom but burdening you with responsibility.
Although your heart's desires are more
changeable once Venus enters fickle Gemini
on **April 25**, you've had enough of the emotional roller coaster, and you want the ride
to end. Push comes to shove on **April 26**
when serious Saturn's long-term opposition
to anything-goes Uranus brings you right to
the edge. Breathe deeply and move slowly, for
conscious action will surely bring better
results than recklessness.

MAY

READY TO FLY

Following your dreams may seem impossible now that stifling Saturn is retrograding back into your 12th House of Endings. Frustrations linger from Saturn's opposition to wild Uranus—which was exact on **April 26**—and you're unlikely to break free of constraint just yet. You struggle to strike a workable balance between spiritual pursuits and daily responsibilities, especially when Saturn forms an irritating quincunx with escapist Neptune on **May 2**. Be careful how you express your annoyance, for problematic aspects to militant Mars on **May 3-4** can provoke unproductive outbursts of anger.

Meanwhile, retrograde Mercury garbles communication and makes it more difficult to get your point across until it turns direct in your 8th House of Deep Sharing on **May 11**. The practical Taurus New Moon on **May 13** accentuates this significant shift, making you more determined than ever to do the inner work that will let you clean up your outer life. But an opposition between expansive Jupiter in your 6th House of Self-Improvement and restrictive Saturn builds to a crescendo on **May 23**, again confronting you with the gulf between your optimistic plans for the future and the unfinished business of the past. Nevertheless, you are standing at the edge of a great shift. Fortunately, you could receive an unexpected push from someone else when surprising Uranus enters enterprising Aries and your 7th House of Others on **May 27**—the same day as the farsighted Sagittarius Full Moon in your 3rd House of Learning. Keep your eyes on the horizon, for you now have the vision you need to successfully make the leap to the future.

KEEP IN MIND THIS MONTH

Instead of going to extremes, find balance by standing between the forces that draw you back into your past and those that pull you forward into your future.

KEY DATES

★ **MAY 2–4**
uncertainty principle
On **May 2**, a long-lasting aspect between somber
Saturn and nebulous Neptune diminishes your
creativity, dampens your spirit, and leaves you
confused. This unsettling quincunx, which recurs
on **June 27**, muddles your judgment about
whether your life is heading in the direction you
want. Persistence enables you to uncover the
hidden agenda of someone who may be working
against your best interests when intelligent
Mercury harmonizes with probing Pluto on **May 3**.
Frustration mounts and acrimony can turn into
open conflict as the purposeful Sun in stubborn
Taurus squares irate Mars on **May 4**. Fortunately,
your peacekeeping skills help you stand up for
your values without doing battle.

★ **MAY 7**
all the right moves
The cosmic lovers, Venus and Mars, meet in a
cooperative sextile that emboldens you to act so
charmingly, you may just get what you want. This

sweet aspect bodes well for romantic or financial interactions; even a fun group activity is memorable with Mars in your 11th House of Friends and Venus in your 9th House of Adventure.

★ **MAY 13**
alchemical shift
Today's Taurus New Moon falls in your 8th House of Intimacy and Transformation, indicating that others have a personal investment in your emotional struggle. Earthy Taurus doesn't like quick change, so choose a more conservative route to explore your feelings within the context of a deepening commitment. A current relationship can be revitalized by a mutual agreement to change within acknowledged boundaries. Mercury the Messenger is also in steady Taurus now and its ongoing trine to evolutionary Pluto reinforces the theme of slow but complete metamorphosis.

SUPER NOVA DAYS

★ **MAY 17–19**
falling in and out of love
When your ruling planet, Venus, squares opulent Jupiter, severe Saturn, and erratic Uranus

in a three-day period, you're bound to experience alternating waves of indulgence and
restraint, along with a few surprises.
Additionally, Venus in your 9th House of Big
Ideas trines fantasy-prone Neptune on **May 18**,
fueling dreams of love. You may be ready for a
last playful fling before Venus leaves flirtatious
Gemini and settles into cautious Cancer and
your professional 10th House on **May 19**.

★ **MAY 23–27**
flipping the switch
Your desire for peace stands between you and
freedom as karmic Saturn in your 12th House of
Destiny is opposed by opportunistic Jupiter on
May 23. Venus's opposition to fierce Pluto won't
let you have a casual attitude about anything
that blocks your way. The Sagittarius Full Moon
on **May 27** connects with Uranus the Awakener
entering fiery Aries, sending shocks through
your nervous system and activating new circuits
to swiftly transport you into the future.

JUNE

QUANTUM LEAP

You are finally free from the oppression of daily details now that electric Uranus is in enthusiastic Aries and your 7th House of Relationships. On **June 6**, confident Jupiter also leaves the confinement of your 6th House of Daily Routines to enter the more spontaneous world of Aries and your 7th House. Jupiter and Uranus form a breakthrough conjunction on **June 8** that sets the tone for upcoming months, when unusual people open your mind to exciting new ways of interacting. Old beliefs—however comfortable and useful—fall away as you're shocked and amazed by unorthodox ideas you once found too radical. But even as your horizons are being broadened, energetic Mars slips into quiet Virgo and your 12th House of Privacy on **June 7**; there he'll remain until **July 29**. On a grand scale, your life is being propelled forward and outward, yet you might feel so overwhelmed that you want to go into hiding or flee to a spiritual retreat.

The New Moon in dualistic Gemini on **June 12** presents you with more professional options than you can pursue. When stylish Venus prances into courageous Leo and your social 11th House on **June 14**—remaining there until **July 10**—you're ready to show the world your warm and expressive side. Your confidence wanes, though, as the Moon waxes full to a Lunar Eclipse on **June 26**. Although this Capricorn Full Moon is conjunct mighty Pluto, the long-term Saturn-Neptune quincunx on **June 27** can temporarily take the wind out of your sails, leaving you uncertain about what to do next.

KEEP IN MIND THIS MONTH

Don't resist the current changes in your life, even if they're chock-full of contradictions. Taking a calculated risk now makes sense.

KEY DATES

★ **JUNE 1–2**
in your mind's eye
The mercurial Gemini Sun forms a magical quintile to joyful Jupiter and eye-opening Uranus, allowing you to imagine the amazing transitions that are about to unfold. Your vision of the future is a dynamic catalyst for change, so make a commitment to use the power of positive thought as a way to catapult your life ahead.

SUPER NOVA DAYS

★ **JUNE 4–8**
and the verdict is . . .
It's hard to know which way to go on **June 4**, when impassioned Mars opposes diffusive Neptune's distorting mirror. Nevertheless, seeds planted when visionary Jupiter joins futuristic Uranus on **June 8** can take months to bear fruit. Unfortunately, you need time to think about your options, because Mars creates a nagging quincunx with the Jupiter-Uranus conjunction on **June 7**. It seems like any choice

you make isn't the right one. Fortunately, logical Mercury in sure-footed Taurus harmonizes
with stabilizing Saturn the next day to give you
the benefit of sound judgment.

★ **JUNE 12–15**
irresistible you
The curious Gemini New Moon on **June 12** falls
in your 9th House of Big Ideas, filling your head
with the noise of your own spinning wheels.
Even if you try to minimize your needs, you
won't be able to contain yourself on **June 14**
when enthralling Venus enters your 11th House
of Dreams and Wishes while trining an irre-
pressible Jupiter-Uranus conjunction. Don't
hold back; tell others what you want now, when
your charisma is charming and disarming.
You're even more convincing thanks to a syner-
getic Mars-Pluto trine on **June 15**, which adds
depth and intensity to everything you do.

★ **JUNE 19–23**
free will reigns
A harsh Sun-Saturn square on **June 19**
requires you to make a critical decision, but

the fuzzy Sun-Neptune trine blurs your choices, making it hard to see the outcome. On the Summer Solstice—**June 21**—the Sun enters your 10th House of Status, nudging you out into the public eye. You know what others want now, yet your actions may not be what they expect. Even if you're under pressure to be responsible, you're still confident enough to do whatever you want when the Sun dances with Jupiter on the **23rd**.

★ **JUNE 26-27**
cut your losses
You must confront an overwhelming amount of change when the serious Capricorn Full Moon Eclipse on **June 26** touches off hard aspects with fast-talking Mercury, judgmental Jupiter, volatile Uranus, and dark Pluto. Don't be too hard on yourself if you don't feel up to the task; a cantankerous Saturn-Neptune quin-cunx may be clouding your judgment. Instead of making apologies, just do the best you can and move on.

JULY

RHYTHM ENTRAINMENT

Your apprehension grows throughout the month, but you may not notice until it's too late to do much about it except deal with the stressors as they arise. The Sun and Mercury in your 10th House of Career are in passive Cancer, tempting you to avoid confrontation.

Although talkative Mercury urges you to speak your mind when it enters outgoing Leo on **July 9**, Venus slips out of Leo and into timid Virgo and your 12th House of Escapism on **July 10**, continuing the theme of evading conflict in relationships. Even assertive Mars loses punch now that he, too, is lost in your 12th House in Virgo until **July 29**. The Solar Eclipse on **July 11** can shift the energy, but you need to pay extra attention or you could miss important clues. This powerful New Moon Eclipse in Cancer can leave you emotionally distraught, especially if you attempt to bury your feelings behind a wall of silence. Yet it also shatters protective boundaries, revealing unexpressed vulnerability that, in turn, leads to closer connections to heal your heart.

When no-nonsense Saturn returns to your sign on **July 21**—after a reprieve that began when it backed into Virgo on **April 7**—you can no longer put off the inevitable. The Sun's entry into loud Leo on **July 22** escalates the action through **July 25**, when the Aquarius Full Moon occurs in your 5th House of Self-Expression. You may struggle, however, to contain your intensity and restrain your ambition as giant Jupiter squares impassioned Pluto on **July 25**. An unrelenting Saturn-Uranus opposition the next day catalyzes dynamic shifts in your closest relationships.

KEEP IN MIND THIS MONTH

Although you may downplay what's happening, events now will continue to grab your attention until you're fully participating in creating your life.

KEY DATES

★ **JULY 3–5**

follow your instincts

Mental Mercury in your 10th House of Career
requires you to talk about your professional
goals, but it's hard for you to be objective when
the Trickster planet is in emotional Cancer.
Luckily, you can use your subjectivity to your
advantage when Mercury magically connects
with skillful Saturn on **July 3** and with fanciful
Neptune on **July 5**. Gathering and analyzing
data won't help you now. Trust your creativity
and your intuition.

★ **JULY 8–9**

take a chance on love

You're in the middle of a tug-of-war when
beautiful Venus and illusory Neptune form an
opposition on **July 8**. Your dream of ideal love
seems within reach, and when messenger
Mercury enters showy Leo on **July 9**, you
can talk unabashedly about your desires.
Additionally, an out-of-the-box Mercury-
Uranus trine rewards originality if you're

willing to risk emotional safety for a chance at
sweet romance.

★ **JULY 13**
in pursuit of pleasure
Stylish Venus may be fussier than usual now
that she's in discriminating Virgo, but your key
planet is also getting lots of green lights from
euphoric Jupiter, encouraging you to go for
whatever your heart desires. Fortunately, Venus
also trines intense Pluto, fueling your drive for
pleasure with a deeper need for a passionate
connection. Light and easy interactions won't
hold your interest very long now unless you can
also make heart-to-heart contact.

★ **JULY 21–23**
the pressure's on
Authoritative Saturn entered Libra on **October 29,
2009**, initiating a process of change that has
seen you take new responsibility for your life.
Although you've had a few months to catch
your breath, the weight of the world returns
when Saturn reenters your sign on **July 21**. A
supportive Sun-Saturn sextile on **July 22** helps

you make mature choices, and its easy trine to progressive Uranus on the **23rd** prevents you from slipping back into old patterns just because they worked before. You may not get there overnight, but you are being steadily pushed into your future.

SUPER NOVA DAYS

★ **JULY 25–26**
freedom of choice

On **July 25**, overconfident Jupiter locks into a square with ruthless Pluto that lasts until **August 3**, propelling you forward on a tidal wave of ambition. Be cautious; you could be so sure you're on the right track, you don't take anyone else's feelings into consideration as you hurdle toward your goals. The eccentric Aquarius Full Moon supports your efforts with quirky originality when the Sun and Moon harmonize with Jupiter. Meanwhile, the Saturn-Uranus opposition on **July 26** could force you to take drastic measures to resolve the relationship tension once and for all.

AUGUST

ALTERNATING CURRENTS

This month is a study in contrasts as indicated by jolly Jupiter and serious Saturn. Your confidence abounds and you're ready to fly, only to discover that your wings have been clipped and you're grounded. This dance of expansion and contraction can impact your life in several different areas, yet Saturn in your 1st House of Self opposes Jupiter in your 7th House of Partners, turning relationships into the main stage for this cosmic drama. Although the Jupiter-Saturn opposition is exact on **August 16**, you'll feel its push–pull effects all month. Meanwhile, motivational Mars is in your sign until **September 14**, boosting your drive to accomplish as much as possible.

Your key planet, Venus, is at home in Libra from **August 6 through September 8**, giving you an extra dose of style and grace. Nevertheless, Mars and Venus each encounter similar restraint from Saturn, encouragement from Jupiter, and a few surprises from shocking Uranus and transformational Pluto from **July 30 to August 10**. Wide swings of emotion will be particularly apparent to others on **August 9**, when the dramatic Leo New

Moon falls in your 11th House of Friends and Associates.

Then—as if it weren't tricky enough sorting through all the conflicting information—Mercury takes a retrograde turn in analytical Virgo on **August 20** to befuddle things even more. You may wonder if you're up for the starring role in your own life when unyielding Saturn squares Pluto on **August 21**, and circumstances limit your ability to make the changes you crave. Fortunately, a psychic Pisces Full Moon on **August 24** gains perspective from incisive Pluto, igniting your intuition and empowering you to make the decisions that will move you forward.

KEEP IN MIND THIS MONTH

When storms of change swirl around you, it's your job to find your way back to the center where you can maintain your balance and catch your breath.

KEY DATES

★ **AUGUST 3–4**
watch your back
You are riding the wave of prosperous Jupiter's
square to ruthless Pluto, which began on **July 25**
and culminates on **August 3**. With Jupiter in
your 7th House of Companions, someone may
offer you an opportunity; when hard-driving
Mars enters the picture on **August 4**, you're
ready to go ahead with the deal. Don't exhaust
yourself by engaging in needless power struggles before reaching your goal.

SUPER NOVA DAYS

★ **AUGUST 7–10**
hold on to your heart
You could fall in love hard and fast with
someone who suddenly appears in your life
on **August 7**, when romantic Venus opposes
unorthodox Uranus in your 7th House of
Others. But reality settles in as Venus joins
sobering Saturn on **August 8**. Fortunately, you
can turn a difficult situation into a beautiful one
the next day, as Venus opposes opulent Jupiter.

103

Simultaneously, the effusive Leo New Moon encourages you to share your feelings. Being vulnerable allows intimacy to grow when Venus squares passionate Pluto on **August 10**. Regardless of the outcome, you will be emotionally richer for having had this experience.

★ **AUGUST 16**
stuck in the middle with you
You're stretched to the max today as Jupiter and Saturn pull at you from opposite directions. This aspect began on **May 23** and repeats on **March 28, 2011**, making today's occurrence a turning point in a much larger transition that has you carefully weighing and balancing the pros and cons of your relationships. Although you may want to make definitive decisions, choices made now will need reconsideration prior to next spring.

★ **AUGUST 21**
pushing through it
You can't escape the heaviness of today's Saturn-Pluto square—the last in a series that began on **November 15, 2009**. Although your

head may be in the clouds, serious demands
are being made upon you and you have no
choice but to act responsibly. Giving up is not
a viable option, yet eliminating excess can
help you focus your attention on what's
most important.

★ **AUGUST 23–26**
soul food
The emotional Pisces Full Moon on **August 24**
falls in your 6th House of Self-Improvement,
suggesting that your feelings can help you navigate through these power-packed days. The
Sun's annoying quincunx with pompous Jupiter
indicates that you might not want to follow the
advice of others, who may encourage you to
risk more than you need. Luckily, your keen
intuition will guide you with a mix of faith and
focus as the Sun in your 12th House of Destiny
trines regenerative Pluto on **August 26**.

SEPTEMBER

CHANGE WILL DO YOU GOOD

This month starts quietly with messenger Mercury retrograde in your 12th House of Endings until **September 12**. Feelings intensify as sensual Venus and ardent Mars leave your even-keeled air sign for the deeper passions of mysterious Scorpio on **September 8 and September 14**, respectively. Your forays into unknown emotional territory are affirmed as giant Jupiter backs into watery Pisces on **September 9** to conjunct unorthodox Uranus on **September 18** in your 6th House of Health and Work. This mind-opening conjunction is the second in a series of three that began on **June 8** and culminates on **January 4, 2011**. Paradoxically, the first one was in your 7th House of Others, placing the focus directly on relationships. Now, however, you are being given an opportunity to alter your perspective on the practical details of your everyday life. Change is no longer just a good idea; it's imperative to break free of restrictive patterns and outmoded habits. Make adjustments to your diet, your exercise program, your job—anywhere you can positively impact your daily routine.

The meticulous Virgo New Moon on **September 8** falls in your spiritual 12th House, juxtaposing your insatiable need for tangible facts with a longing to discover the true purpose of your soul. You become acutely aware of the vast differences between your inner world and the outer one when the Sun opposes Jupiter and Uranus on **September 21**. Your task is to restore balance to your life, especially around the Fall Equinox, because the Sun enters Libra the Scales on **September 22**. Your negotiating skills are called into action on **September 23**, when the insistent Aries Full Moon pushes you to resolve previously hidden tensions.

KEEP IN MIND THIS MONTH

Although you're naturally more comfortable operating in a rational manner, it may be time to leave logic behind and learn to trust your feelings.

KEY DATES

★ **SEPTEMBER 4**
temporary reprieve
An easy trine between romantic Venus and
otherworldly Neptune can serve up a dreamy
day. You make others feel special, yet you may
be so sensitive to them that you forget about
your own needs. The good news is that you can
be happy no matter what happens, for your
fantasies trump reality now. The bad news is
that the rose-colored glasses won't always
keep your daydreams from crashing to earth.

★ **SEPTEMBER 7–9**
love hangover
Venus tempts you with the possibility of
immediate gratification when she forms
a tricky quincunx with subversive Uranus on
September 7. The New Moon in precise Virgo
on **September 8** normally clears the air of
cloudy illusions, but sultry Venus encourages
secrecy when she enters enigmatic Scorpio on
the same day. It's hard to know how best to
express your desires now. Physical Mars forms

a superconductive trine with mystical Neptune on **September 9**, further complicating your life. This magical connection can be fun, but it might be wiser to take the high road and choose spiritual love over personal indulgence.

★ **SEPTEMBER 12-13**
keep it simple
Cerebral Mercury turns direct on **September 12**, but you may find intellectual solutions more workable in theory than in practice when action-oriented Mars forms an unmanageable quincunx with the explosive Jupiter-Uranus conjunction on **September 13**. It's a struggle for you to manage your physical energy now—you're tempted to do either too much or too little. Eliminating excess noise and getting back to the basics is your best strategy at the moment.

SUPER NOVA DAYS

★ **SEPTEMBER 18-23**
it's all too much
Global Jupiter joins irreverent Uranus on **September 18** to shake and wake you up. You see your life in a different light now, and you

can't return to the past. Your horizons continue
to expand through the Sun's illuminating
opposition to Jupiter and Uranus on
September 21. Although you may feel like
you're standing still, it's just because the tides
are changing direction. The Sun 's move into
your sign on the **22nd** mixed with the irre-
pressible Aries Full Moon in your 7th House of
Partners on the **23rd** marks the height of this
powerful shift and can aim you in an entirely
new direction, although it may take a while yet
to see where you will land.

★ **SEPTEMBER 30**
do the right thing
The sobering Sun-Saturn conjunction falls in
your sign, demanding a higher level of self-
discipline. Even if you attempt to avoid responsibilities now, they will haunt you, and you'll
still need to deliver what you promised. It's
easier, however, if you fulfill your obligations
on your own, rather than waiting for circumstances to force you to do the right thing.

OCTOBER

THE ROAD NOT TAKEN

You are cautious as the month begins, yet a surge of creativity feeds your optimism, encouraging you to overcome recent obstacles. Your discretion comes from the Sun's proximity to conservative Saturn in your fair-minded sign, yet it quickly gives way to marvelous possibilities brought by Mercury's connection with self-assured Jupiter and ingenious Uranus on **October 1 and 2**. By **October 3**, when Mercury slips into Libra, your objectivity helps you maintain your cool while responding to unexpected twists and turns in your chosen path. The ambivalent Libra New Moon on **October 7** is like your personal New Year's Day, reflecting your desire to make balanced choices that are best for everyone. You are hesitant to decide one way or another because you can see potential in both options.

Your key planet, Venus, turns retrograde in your 2nd House of Self-Worth on **October 8** to complicate matters and rattle your confidence. Although time marches on, your heart turns backward and inward in search of happiness, lost love, or buried treasure. You can't recapture the past, but revisiting it can help you make the most of the present on **November 18**, when Venus resumes its direct motion. It's time to bring a relationship issue to the front burner when a friend or lover confronts you in a way that agitates you on **October 22** as the self-centered Aries Full Moon falls in your 7th House of Partners. Your first choice might be to acquiesce, yet the Sun's entry into driven Scorpio on **October 23**—where it joins Mercury, Venus, and Mars—arms you with commitment to your own agenda, making you less willing to compromise.

KEEP IN MIND THIS MONTH

Even if your happiness depends on those around you, don't be too quick to relinquish your desires in favor of someone else's demands.

KEY DATES

★ **OCTOBER 1–4**
all or nothing
Instead of surrendering as life get tough, inspire yourself with your vision of what the future may bring. Imagining the best-case scenario is easy on **October 1**, when mental Mercury receives an encouraging boost from Jupiter. Mercury's opposition to reactionary Uranus the next day requires you to make a quantum leap, perhaps revealing your feelings to someone special. A sexy Venus-Mars conjunction in seductive Scorpio on **October 3** can bring passion in the romance or finance department, but an unpredictable Mars-Uranus hookup on **October 4** can increase the sizzle—or instantly break the connection.

★ **OCTOBER 7–9**
desperately seeking something
It's hard to decide what image to present or even to know what you want on **October 7**, when the New Moon in ambiguous Libra temporarily dampens your social life. You long to

see yourself in the mirror of someone else's soul, but may not find anyone to meet you at this profound level. Communicator Mercury aligns with stern Saturn on **October 8**—the same day that sweet Venus starts her backward dance in your 2nd House of Values. If you don't have to deal with disapproval from someone you respect, you might be your own harshest critic. A diffusive Mercury-Neptune alignment on **October 9** now offers you an escape route from an unpleasant set of circumstances.

SUPER NOVA DAYS

★ OCTOBER 18–20
spinning yarns
Relief arrives at your doorstep in many guises now, yet each of them contains the common element of fantasy as clever Mercury and the Sun harmoniously hook up with whimsical Neptune on **October 18 and 19**. With Mercury and the Sun in your 1st House of Personality, you can project your dreams onto others. Problems arise, however, from the juxtaposition of fiction and fact **October 19–20** when Mercury and the Sun create unmanageable

quincunxes with unpredictable Uranus in your practical 6th House. Fortunately, a flamboyant Mars-Jupiter trine on **October 20** enables you to make a grandiose gesture that puts others at ease. Your gracious approach easily covers what you don't know while you're making up the rest.

★ **OCTOBER 27–28**
mood swings
Solemn Saturn in your sign rubs up against nebulous Neptune in your 5th House of Self-Expression on **October 27**, inducing free-floating anxiety or melancholy. You may struggle with recent decisions, wondering where you'd be now if you'd made different choices. But your malaise doesn't last, for motivating Mars enters adventurous Sagittarius on the **28th** to put your life back on the move. The Sun's conjunction with beautiful Venus in your 2nd House of Self-Worth sweetens the picture by inspiring you to invest in your own pleasure.

NOVEMBER

THE THINGS WE DO FOR LOVE

Your ambivalence falls away this month as you see farther into your future and make choices with more certainty. The New Moon in transformative Scorpio on **November 6** falls in your 2nd House of Money and Resources, focusing your attention on practical matters that affect your income and your material wealth. You need to be a financial detective as you gather information to overcome logical Mercury's confusing square to elusive Neptune. However, having the right data allows you to intuitively draw conclusions when the sudden awareness of Mercury's trine to Uranus clears the air of any muddled thoughts. Yet you don't feel like you're getting any closer to your heart's desire because your ruling planet, Venus, continues a retrograde period that began on **October 8**. When sweet Venus backs into artistic Libra and your 1st House of Personality on **November 7**, you may feel especially creative, stylish, and alluring.

An uneasy dissonance between Venus's indulgent desire for pleasure and your personal need for freedom is exaggerated all month by Mars in idealistic Sagittarius. Emotional satisfaction may elude you until romantic Venus turns direct on **November 18**—yet even then you may be required to surrender more than you wish. The Full Moon in back-to-basics Taurus on **November 21** falls in your 8th House of Intimacy and Transformation, helping you find your place in the new emotional landscape. The Sun's entry into inspirational Sagittarius on **November 22**, followed by dynamic squares to boundless Jupiter from Mercury on **November 25** and Mars on **November 29**, dares you to go beyond your normal limits and reach for your dreams.

KEEP IN MIND THIS MONTH

No matter how sure you are that beauty is fleeting, truth evasive, and happiness elusive, don't give in— true satisfaction lurks just around the corner.

KEY DATES

★ **NOVEMBER 4–6**
nothing ventured, nothing gained
You may receive good news at work on
November 4 when Mercury the Messenger
slides into a harmonious trine with generous
Jupiter in your 6th House of Employment.
Mercury in penetrating Scorpio is in your 2nd
House of Income, so what you learn might
help you make more money. The Scorpio New
Moon on **November 6** intensifies your concen-
tration, enabling you to follow through on your
intentions. Mercury's fortunate trine to brilliant
Uranus on the same day indicates that a risk
will likely bring surprising rewards.

★ **NOVEMBER 7–8**
contagious charisma
There is a change in your attitude when
resourceful Venus retrogrades into creative
Libra on **November 7**—she remains in your 1st
House of Self until **November 29**—giving you
more clarity in your decisions about love and
money. Venus forms a beautiful biquintile with

opulent Jupiter on **November 8**, painting your world with pleasing possibilities. Interactive Mercury's move into gregarious Sagittarius and your 3rd House of Immediate Environment increases your ability to convince your closest friends, neighbors, and co-workers that your optimistic outlook has merit and your ideas are worth pursuing.

★ **NOVEMBER 15**
make it so
You expect a favorable outcome from a difficult situation at work now that the Sun harmoniously trines upbeat Jupiter. This isn't idle daydreaming, for assertive Mars receives support from persistent Saturn, providing you with the organizational savvy necessary to conceive a concrete plan and the physical endurance to make it happen.

SUPER NOVA DAYS

★ **NOVEMBER 19–22**
into the wild blue yonder
An innovative Sun-Uranus trine on **November 19** suddenly reveals a solution to a puzzling

NOVEMBER   ♎

problem. Luckily, a Mercury-Mars conjunction in your information-rich 3rd House the next day gives you the words and the delivery that inspire others to follow, even if you meet some justifiable resistance. The stable Taurus Full Moon on **November 21** helps you hold on to your position when the Sun enters grandiose Sagittarius on **November 22**, tempting you to bite off more than you can chew. A little self-restraint goes a long way toward getting you to your distant goal.

★ **NOVEMBER 29–30**
  downsize it
  Once again, the temptation of promising too much at work can get you into hot water when go-getter Mars squares overblown Jupiter on **November 29**. Venus's entry into survivalist Scorpio the same day helps you regain focus, and Mercury's entry into traditional Capricorn and your 4th House of Foundations on **November 30** can quickly bring your ideas back down to size.

DECEMBER

MAKE IT WORK

Behind all the thrills and spills this month is your drive toward the third and final conjunction of inspirational Jupiter and breakthrough Uranus in your 6th House of Self-Improvement. Ideas and opportunities that first appeared on **June 8 and September 18** cycle around again, and although this alignment isn't exact until **January 4, 2011**, the anticipation mounts throughout the month. Still, potent Pluto in controlling Capricorn and your 4th House of Domestic Conditions can strengthen your emotions and intensify struggles with family members—especially when it's joined by communicator Mercury on **December 5**, by Mercury and Mars on **December 13**, and by the Sun on **December 26**.

Mercury's retrograde period **December 10–30** begins in your 4th House, exposing unexpressed tensions at home, and then backs into cavalier Sagittarius and your 3rd House of Information on **December 18**, tempting you to avoid difficult conversations in favor of more enjoyable activities. This bodes well for the holiday season, but friendly Venus in emotional Scorpio all month reminds you that lighthearted fun is not a replacement for the deeper connections of the heart—and they aren't always simple or straightforward. Your high ideals inspire you onward as a New Moon in philosophical Sagittarius on **December 5** raises your spirits, but it's in your 3rd House of Immediate Environment, suggesting the need to act locally while thinking globally. The restless Gemini Full Moon on **December 21** is a Lunar Eclipse on the same day as the Winter Solstice. This powerful combo acts as a catalyst. Your intense reactions to your own inner truth can drive hidden emotions out into the open and force you to deal with the consequences of expressing your feelings.

KEEP IN MIND THIS MONTH

Expect a few personal struggles during the holiday season—and remember that they'll soon be put into perspective by the big changes just ahead.

KEY DATES

★ **DECEMBER 1-3**
unexpected results
Although you naturally express yourself with
great ease, you aren't interested in witty
banter now. Instead, you need to talk about
an issue that is fundamental to your beliefs.
Fortunately, you can broach this sensitive topic
gently when aggressive Mars is subdued by
a sextile to diluted Neptune on **December 2**.
Still, what you say will have consequences—
and Mars's explosive square to wired Uranus
on **December 3** can elicit a surprising reaction.

★ **DECEMBER 5**
heart of darkness
Your high expectations of love are brought out
into the open by today's spirited Sagittarius
New Moon. Yet you also need to talk about
your deepest fears when verbal Mercury conjuncts mysterious Pluto, beginning a process
that transforms veiled negative emotions into
shared positive ones. Shining the light of consciousness into the shadows of subconscious

motivation is painful, yet it rewards you with knowledge about your soul.

★ **DECEMBER 12–15**
metaphysical bounty
A superconjunction of the soulful Lunar North Node, red-hot Mars, tyrannical Pluto, and mischievous Mercury turns these days into a transformational cauldron of alchemical change. This alignment occurs in your private 4th House of Security, rocking the foundations of your emotional world by stirring domestic struggles based on nearly forgotten issues from your past. You may not enjoy untangling labyrinthine family politics, but the process can recover buried treasures that are true gifts of this holiday season.

SUPER NOVA DAYS

★ **DECEMBER 18–21**
supersize it
Your overactive imagination puts you in a festive mood on **December 18** when a spiritual Sun-Neptune sextile opens your mind wide. Aspects to wild and crazy Uranus, combined

with Mercury's entry to farsighted Sagittarius,
make it easy to transform gloom into glee. But
if you get carried away by your exhilaration,
the unstable Gemini Full Moon Eclipse on
December 21 can throw you for a loop. This
eclipse falls in your 9th House of Higher Truth
and will let you know if you're misleading yourself about your direction in life. It's important
to pare back your plans, for Mercury's square
to unrestrained Jupiter may have you running
around in circles without making any progress.

★ **DECEMBER 26–30**
at the end of your rope
An intense Sun-Pluto conjunction on
December 26 has you revisiting communication issues first raised on **December 5** when
Mercury connected with unrelenting Pluto. But
insistent Mars's square to parental Saturn in
your 1st House of Self on **December 29** says
enough is enough. No matter how old you are,
it's time to grow up. Stop dancing, turn off the
music, and get serious about the commitments you're making.

APPENDIXES

★

2010 MONTH-AT-A-GLANCE ASTROCALENDAR

★

FAMOUS LIBRANS

★

LIBRA IN LOVE

FRIDAY 1 ★ It's hard to tell where your fantasies end and reality begins

SATURDAY 2 ★

SUNDAY 3

MONDAY 4

TUESDAY 5

WEDNESDAY 6

THURSDAY 7 ★ Trust your feelings and reach outside of the box for solutions

FRIDAY 8 ★

SATURDAY 9 ★

SUNDAY 10 ★

MONDAY 11 ★

TUESDAY 12

WEDNESDAY 13 ★ Uncharacteristic impatience prompts you to take a chance

THURSDAY 14 ★

FRIDAY 15 ★ ●

SATURDAY 16

SUNDAY 17

MONDAY 18

TUESDAY 19

WEDNESDAY 20

THURSDAY 21

FRIDAY 22 ★ This is a good time for a business deal or intimate agreement

SATURDAY 23

SUNDAY 24

MONDAY 25

TUESDAY 26

WEDNESDAY 27 ★ **SUPER NOVA DAYS** Your needs clash with those around you

THURSDAY 28 ★

FRIDAY 29 ★

SATURDAY 30 ★ ○

SUNDAY 31 ★

★ designates key date

MONDAY 1

TUESDAY 2 ★ It's time to address powerful emotions in your
relationships now

WEDNESDAY 3

THURSDAY 4

FRIDAY 5 ★ Give yourself permission to want more than you have

SATURDAY 6 ★

SUNDAY 7 ★

MONDAY 8 ★

TUESDAY 9

WEDNESDAY 10 ★ A friend or associate may misinterpret your impulsive actions

THURSDAY 11 ★

FRIDAY 12 ★

SATURDAY 13 ★ ●

SUNDAY 14

MONDAY 15

TUESDAY 16   SUPER NOVA DAYS It's hard to avoid falling in love

WEDNESDAY 17 ★

THURSDAY 18 ★

FRIDAY 19

SATURDAY 20

SUNDAY 21

MONDAY 22

TUESDAY 23

WEDNESDAY 24

THURSDAY 25

FRIDAY 26

SATURDAY 27   ○

SUNDAY 28 ★ Opportunity is knocking; you'd be wise to let it in

MONDAY 1

TUESDAY 2

WEDNESDAY 3 ★ You could make choices that seem out of character

THURSDAY 4 ★

FRIDAY 5

SATURDAY 6

SUNDAY 7 ★ **SUPER NOVA DAYS** Be careful what you ask for, because you just might get it

MONDAY 8 ★

TUESDAY 9 ★

WEDNESDAY 10 ★

THURSDAY 11 ★

FRIDAY 12

SATURDAY 13

SUNDAY 14

MONDAY 15 ★ ● Plant seeds of intention to turn a good idea into daily practice

TUESDAY 16

WEDNESDAY 17 ★ New people enter your life to propel you forward

THURSDAY 18 ★

FRIDAY 19 ★

SATURDAY 20 ★

SUNDAY 21 ★

MONDAY 22 ★

TUESDAY 23

WEDNESDAY 24

THURSDAY 25

FRIDAY 26

SATURDAY 27

SUNDAY 28

MONDAY 29 ○

TUESDAY 30

WEDNESDAY 31

THURSDAY 1	
FRIDAY 2	
SATURDAY 3 ★	You take discussions of love into vulnerable, meaningful places

SUNDAY 4 ★	
MONDAY 5 ★	
TUESDAY 6 ★	
WEDNESDAY 7	
THURSDAY 8	
FRIDAY 9	
SATURDAY 10 ★	Well-meaning friends could be the source of annoyance now

SUNDAY 11	
MONDAY 12	
TUESDAY 13	
WEDNESDAY 14 ●	
THURSDAY 15	
FRIDAY 16	
SATURDAY 17 ★	Learn what you can by revisiting recent love lessons

SUNDAY 18 ★	
MONDAY 19	
TUESDAY 20	
WEDNESDAY 21	
THURSDAY 22 ★	SUPER NOVA DAYS Breathe deeply and move slowly; conscious action is better than recklessness

FRIDAY 23 ★	
SATURDAY 24 ★	
SUNDAY 25 ★	
MONDAY 26 ★	
TUESDAY 27	
WEDNESDAY 28 ○	
THURSDAY 29	
FRIDAY 30	

SATURDAY 1

SUNDAY 2 ★ You uncover someone's hidden agenda

MONDAY 3 ★

TUESDAY 4 ★

WEDNESDAY 5

THURSDAY 6

FRIDAY 7 ★ You assert yourself so charmingly that you may get what you want

SATURDAY 8

SUNDAY 9

MONDAY 10

TUESDAY 11

WEDNESDAY 12

THURSDAY 13 ★ ● Others have a personal investment in your
emotional struggle

FRIDAY 14

SATURDAY 15

SUNDAY 16

MONDAY 17 ★ SUPER NOVA DAYS You're torn between indulgence and restraint

TUESDAY 18 ★

WEDNESDAY 19 ★

THURSDAY 20

FRIDAY 21

SATURDAY 22

SUNDAY 23 ★ Your desire for peace stands between you and freedom

MONDAY 24 ★

TUESDAY 25 ★

WEDNESDAY 26 ★

THURSDAY 27 ★ ○

FRIDAY 28

SATURDAY 29

SUNDAY 30

MONDAY 31

TUESDAY 1 ★ Use positive thought to catapult your life ahead

WEDNESDAY 2 ★

THURSDAY 3

FRIDAY 4 ★ **SUPER NOVA DAYS** You need time to think about your options

SATURDAY 5 ★

SUNDAY 6 ★

MONDAY 7 ★

TUESDAY 8 ★

WEDNESDAY 9

THURSDAY 10

FRIDAY 11

SATURDAY 12 ★ ● Don't hold back; tell others what you want now

SUNDAY 13 ★

MONDAY 14 ★

TUESDAY 15 ★

WEDNESDAY 16

THURSDAY 17

FRIDAY 18

SATURDAY 19 ★ You are required to make a critical decision

SUNDAY 20 ★

MONDAY 21 ★

TUESDAY 22 ★

WEDNESDAY 23 ★

THURSDAY 24

FRIDAY 25

SATURDAY 26 ★ ○ Instead of making apologies, just do the best you can

SUNDAY 27 ★

MONDAY 28

TUESDAY 29

WEDNESDAY 30

THURSDAY 1

FRIDAY 2

SATURDAY 3 ★ Trust your creativity and your intuition

SUNDAY 4 ★

MONDAY 5 ★

TUESDAY 6

WEDNESDAY 7

THURSDAY 8 ★ Your dream of ideal love seems within reach

FRIDAY 9 ★

SATURDAY 10

SUNDAY 11 ●

MONDAY 12

TUESDAY 13 ★ Go for whatever your heart desires

WEDNESDAY 14

THURSDAY 15

FRIDAY 16

SATURDAY 17

SUNDAY 18

MONDAY 19

TUESDAY 20

WEDNESDAY 21 ★ The weight of the world returns today

THURSDAY 22 ★

FRIDAY 23 ★

SATURDAY 24

SUNDAY 25 ★ ○ SUPER NOVA DAYS Be cautious against overconfidence

MONDAY 26 ★

TUESDAY 27

WEDNESDAY 28

THURSDAY 29

FRIDAY 30

SATURDAY 31

SUNDAY 1

MONDAY 2

TUESDAY 3 ★ Don't exhaust yourself by engaging in needless power struggles

WEDNESDAY 4 ★

THURSDAY 5

FRIDAY 6

SATURDAY 7 ★ SUPER NOVA DAYS You could fall in love hard and fast

SUNDAY 8 ★

MONDAY 9 ★ ●

TUESDAY 10 ★

WEDNESDAY 11

THURSDAY 12

FRIDAY 13

SATURDAY 14

SUNDAY 15

MONDAY 16 ★ You're stretched to the max today

TUESDAY 17

WEDNESDAY 18

THURSDAY 19

FRIDAY 20

SATURDAY 21 ★ Eliminating clutter can help you focus on what matters

SUNDAY 22

MONDAY 23 ★ You might not want to follow the advice of others

TUESDAY 24 ★ ○

WEDNESDAY 25 ★

THURSDAY 26 ★

FRIDAY 27

SATURDAY 28

SUNDAY 29

MONDAY 30

TUESDAY 31

WEDNESDAY 1

THURSDAY 2

FRIDAY 3

SATURDAY 4 ★ Your fantasies trump reality now

SUNDAY 5

MONDAY 6

TUESDAY 7 ★ Choose spiritual love over personal indulgence

WEDNESDAY 8 ★ ●

THURSDAY 9 ★

FRIDAY 10

SATURDAY 11

SUNDAY 12 ★ Turn off the noise and get back to the basics

MONDAY 13 ★

TUESDAY 14

WEDNESDAY 15

THURSDAY 16

FRIDAY 17

SATURDAY 18 ★ SUPER NOVA DAYS You see your life in a different light, and you can't return to the past

SUNDAY 19 ★

MONDAY 20 ★

TUESDAY 21 ★

WEDNESDAY 22 ★

THURSDAY 23 ★ ○

FRIDAY 24

SATURDAY 25

SUNDAY 26

MONDAY 27

TUESDAY 28

WEDNESDAY 29

THURSDAY 30 ★ You still need to deliver what you promised

FRIDAY 1 ★ Inspire yourself with a vision of what the future may bring

SATURDAY 2 ★

SUNDAY 3 ★

MONDAY 4 ★

TUESDAY 5

WEDNESDAY 6

THURSDAY 7 ★ ● Your social life is temporarily dampened

FRIDAY 8 ★

SATURDAY 9 ★

SUNDAY 10

MONDAY 11

TUESDAY 12

WEDNESDAY 13

THURSDAY 14

FRIDAY 15

SATURDAY 16

SUNDAY 17

MONDAY 18 ★ **SUPER NOVA DAYS** You make a grandiose gesture that puts others at ease

TUESDAY 19 ★

WEDNESDAY 20 ★

THURSDAY 21

FRIDAY 22 ○

SATURDAY 23

SUNDAY 24

MONDAY 25

TUESDAY 26

WEDNESDAY 27 ★ You may struggle with recent decisions

THURSDAY 28 ★

FRIDAY 29

SATURDAY 30

SUNDAY 31

MONDAY 1

TUESDAY 2

WEDNESDAY 3

THURSDAY 4 ★ You may receive good news at work

FRIDAY 5 ★

SATURDAY 6 ★ ●

SUNDAY 7 ★ You have more clarity in your decisions about love and money

MONDAY 8 ★

TUESDAY 9

WEDNESDAY 10

THURSDAY 11

FRIDAY 12

SATURDAY 13

SUNDAY 14

MONDAY 15 ★ Expect a favorable outcome from a difficult situation

TUESDAY 16

WEDNESDAY 17

THURSDAY 18

FRIDAY 19 ★ **SUPER NOVA DAYS** Your words inspire others to follow

SATURDAY 20 ★

SUNDAY 21 ★ ○

MONDAY 22 ★

TUESDAY 23

WEDNESDAY 24

THURSDAY 25

FRIDAY 26

SATURDAY 27

SUNDAY 28

MONDAY 29 ★ The lure of promising too much can get you in trouble

TUESDAY 30 ★

WEDNESDAY 1 ★ You need to talk about an issue fundamental to your beliefs

THURSDAY 2 ★

FRIDAY 3 ★

SATURDAY 4

SUNDAY 5 ★ ● Sharing your deepest fears will yield knowledge

MONDAY 6

TUESDAY 7

WEDNESDAY 8

THURSDAY 9

FRIDAY 10

SATURDAY 11

SUNDAY 12 ★ Domestic struggles based on nearly forgotten issues are stirred

MONDAY 13 ★

TUESDAY 14 ★

WEDNESDAY 15 ★

THURSDAY 16

FRIDAY 17

SATURDAY 18 ★ **SUPER NOVA DAYS** It's important to pare back your plans

SUNDAY 19 ★

MONDAY 20 ★

TUESDAY 21 ★ ○

WEDNESDAY 22

THURSDAY 23

FRIDAY 24

SATURDAY 25

SUNDAY 26 ★ No matter how old you are, it's time to grow up

MONDAY 27 ★

TUESDAY 28 ★

WEDNESDAY 29 ★

THURSDAY 30 ★

FRIDAY 31

FAMOUS LIBRANS

Bruce Springsteen	★	9/23/1949
Ray Charles	★	9/23/1930
Linda McCartney	★	9/24/1941
F. Scott Fitzgerald	★	9/24/1896
Jim Henson	★	9/24/1936
Heather Locklear	★	9/25/1961
Barbara Walters	★	9/25/1929
William Faulkner	★	9/25/1897
Christopher Reeve	★	9/25/1952
Catherine Zeta-Jones	★	9/25/1969
Serena Williams	★	9/26/1981
T. S. Eliot	★	9/26/1888
George Gershwin	★	9/26/1898
Gwyneth Paltrow	★	9/28/1972
Ed Sullivan	★	9/28/1902
Brigitte Bardot	★	9/28/1934
Jerry Lee Lewis	★	9/29/1935
Miguel de Cervantes	★	9/29/1547
Bryant Gumbel	★	9/29/1948
Angie Dickinson	★	9/30/1931
Mark McGwire	★	10/1/1963
Jimmy Carter	★	10/1/1924
Walter Matthau	★	10/1/1920
Donna Karan	★	10/2/1948
Mahatma Gandhi	★	10/2/1869
Sting	★	10/2/1951
Stevie Ray Vaughan	★	10/3/1954
Gore Vidal	★	10/3/1925
Chubby Checker	★	10/3/1941
Buster Keaton	★	10/4/1895
Susan Sarandon	★	10/4/1946
Anne Rice	★	10/4/1941
Grant Hill	★	10/5/1972
Kate Winslet	★	10/5/1975
Mario Lemieux	★	10/5/1965

FAMOUS LIBRANS

Carole Lombard	★	10/6/1908
Yo-Yo Ma	★	10/7/1955
Vladimir Putin	★	10/7/1952
Simon Cowell	★	10/7/1959
Bishop Desmond Tutu	★	10/7/1931
Sigourney Weaver	★	10/8/1949
Jesse Jackson	★	10/8/1941
John Lennon	★	10/9/1940
Helen Hayes	★	10/10/1900
Brett Favre	★	10/10/1969
Thelonious Monk	★	10/10/1917
David Lee Roth	★	10/10/1954
Eleanor Roosevelt	★	10/11/1884
Elmore Leonard	★	10/11/1925
Hugh Jackman	★	10/12/1968
Luciano Pavarotti	★	10/12/1935
Margaret Thatcher	★	10/13/1925
Marie Osmond	★	10/13/1959
Paul Simon	★	10/13/1941
Ralph Lauren	★	10/14/1939
e. e. cummings	★	10/14/1894
Roger Moore	★	10/14/1927
Penny Marshall	★	10/15/1942
Mario Puzo	★	10/15/1920
Flea	★	10/16/1962
Oscar Wilde	★	10/16/1854
Angela Lansbury	★	10/16/1925
Eminem	★	10/17/1972
Rita Hayworth	★	10/17/1918
Wynton Marsalis	★	10/18/1961
Lee Harvey Oswald	★	10/18/1939
Evander Holyfield	★	10/19/1962
Viggo Mortensen	★	10/20/1958
Mickey Mantle	★	10/20/1931
Bela Lugosi	★	10/20/1882
Arthur Rimbaud	★	10/20/1854
Benjamin Netanyahu	★	10/21/1949
Catherine Deneuve	★	10/22/1943

LIBRA IN LOVE

LIBRA–ARIES (MARCH 21–APRIL 19)

You Librans are gracious and easily project your individuality through cooperation with other people. Your personality tends to attract people into your life who can become a mirror to you, helping you gain elusive self-awareness. You carry a strong sense of justice in all your actions as you uphold the equality in your relationships. Aries is your astrological opposite. Aries are less prone to join groups and have less need for harmony in relationships. They're rugged individuals who prefer to work alone, so you'll have to adjust to the extreme differences in character between you and your Aries lover. If, however, the Moon or Mars is in a fire sign in your chart, the differences won't seem so vast and your chances for compatibility are greatly improved. You will have to give your Aries partner a lot of latitude and enough room for independent action. Together, you'll need to find a middle ground that balances Aries' self-interests with your need for mutual sharing. This relationship can work, but don't expect it to be easy. It'll be like riding a see-saw as you go back and forth between your individual styles.

LIBRA-TAURUS (APRIL 20-MAY 20)

You will relish the down-to-earth joy of the Bull.
Both of you love the beauty of nature, art, music,
and design, but your Taurus lover might be more
sensual than you. You tend toward an aesthetic and
aloof personality coupled with a need for balance,
especially in the area of relationships. You strive
toward cooperation, whereas your bull-headed
partner can find it difficult to compromise for the
sake of peace. Their stubbornness can be quite
frustrating to you, for you may feel that you're always
the one who gives in. If, however, the Moon in your
chart is in Taurus, Leo, Scorpio, or Aquarius, you can
become a formidable opponent in negotiations with
your immovable Taurus partner. He or she can offer
you a practical approach to life that is simpler and
more innocent than you have alone. Since both of
you have Venus as your ruling planet, pleasure rules
your roost—though it may be more mental for you
and physical for Taurus. Ultimately, if the two of you
have common values, you can be happy, for neither
of you live outside the perimeters of your morals.
This relationship requires individual adjustments,
but you'll have many a romantic night dreaming
about all the beautiful things you can do together.

LIBRA-GEMINI (MAY 21–JUNE 20)

You can merge with your Gemini into a happy couple—enjoying the beautiful and refined aspects of life. You may struggle to remain focused and grounded together, for as two air signs, you tend toward living in an idealistic world of ideas and dreams that can fail to produce results and practical success in the real world. If either of you have the Moon, Mercury, Venus or Mars in earth signs, you will be better equipped to deal with the day-to-day responsibilities of living. Without other planets in earth signs, yours is a mental relationship, so communication is of key importance to both of you. Your Gemini lover will stimulate your creativity, inspiring you to greater heights of expression. You, on the other hand, will help your clever Gemini to incorporate an artistic grace in what they say or write. Together, you are dreamers and schemers, and will love to delve into the infinite possibilities that lay before you. One romantic aspect of this union may include writing poems, letters, or e-mail to each another and creating lovely things of beauty to give each other as gifts. You may have found yourself a lifelong playmate, lover, and friend, and together you will keep each other young at heart.

LIBRA-CANCER (JUNE 21–JULY 22)

You have high ideals in your relationships and seek to understand your partner as a means to broaden your own self-reflection and identity. Therefore, you may assume a mental stance in a relationship, which is not problematic unless you're with a water sign, such as Cancer. Your Cancer lover is a deeply emotional and highly sensitive person who may be overwhelmed and even perplexed by your detached style. Your Crab prefers to feel their way through a situation, nourishing and protecting those they love with a giving and open heart. No question about it: you appreciate this devotion. On the other hand, you may feel burdened, even claustrophobic, by the ever-present and sometimes unspoken needs of your insecure Cancer lover, unless the Moon or Venus in your chart is in a water sign (Cancer, Scorpio, or Pisces). Your partner is addicted to the comfort that comes through sharing and commitment. In the meantime, you want to understand and think about a mutual union, yet in the end, your actual commitment and steadfast concentration may waver. Needless to say, this will irritate your mate. If you can work out this difference of character, you should be able to love each other with care and respect.

LIBRA–LEO (JULY 23–AUGUST 22)

You are normally not too judgmental, but with your refined sense of beauty you'll either adore Leos or find them totally exasperating. If you are already in a relationship with a Lion, you probably fell on the side of adoration. This is perfect, for your Leo mate needs outward displays of love and affection. Your Lion can bring new friends and social experiences to you, for Leo is generally optimistic and outgoing. And you do enjoy the social events and opportunities to meet new and interesting people. You do, however, have particular tastes that can, at times, seem picky—especially to your Leo partner, who is more concerned with fun and cheer than worrying about being in the wrong social circle. But as long as Leo receives a fair share of attention, things will remain at peace. One issue is that you can feel disdain for showy exploitation. This can be even more of a problem if your Venus is in Virgo or Scorpio. You'll have to open your thinking to allow your partner's friends to enter your life. You will be happier in this fun-loving relationship if you don't try to prune away your Leo's grandiose social life. Give your mate enough room to find amusement and he or she will open your heart in a way you never thought possible.

LIBRA-VIRGO (AUGUST 23–SEPT. 22)

You can have a difficult time making decisions because of your unique ability to see both sides of most situations. Accordingly, you make great mediators. But, unlike the other zodiac signs, you need a constant flow of input from others around you in order to know yourself or others fully. You move back and forth like a see-saw, from idea to idea, until you are externally motivated or forced to make a final decision. This trait will be difficult for Virgos, who are exact and finite about details and life agendas. In fact, you can make them quite crazy. You do enjoy each other's refined individual presentation and probably feel at home when you are around each other. In a daily routine, however, you will find yourself frustrated by your mate's impatience and criticism toward your changing mind. You two make good classmates and can help each other along a course of common study. As romantic partners, however, you're going to need help from compatible placements of your Moon, Venus, and Mars. Even with help from the romantic planets, you'll still need to make solid decisions and stick to agreed-upon commitments for this relationship to last.

LIBRA–LIBRA (SEPT. 23–OCT. 22)

Sometimes a relationship with someone of your own sign is a perfectly wonderful thing. You Librans, however, have an innate willingness to lose yourself in your partner. Put the two of you together, and you may flounder about, for without the presence of a grounding influence, this may be a pie-in-the-sky union without the means to bring it to fruition. Both of you are highly idealistic and artistic. Sure, you can build castles in the sky, but can you bring your relationship down to earth? When you're with another Libra, the placement of the other planets in each of your charts can determine whether you are mutually compatible. In particular, you will need good aspects between the Moon, Venus, and Mars. Regardless of these aspects, you can achieve great success with a Libra lover if you each practice sticking to commitments and making clear decisions that benefit the two of you as well as others. Together, you can enjoy creating music, art, poetry, and clothing, as well as writing love letters and sharing intimate thoughts. This can be a very sweet union, but again, the question arises—can you two stay centered enough to produce the stability needed for the long haul?

LIBRA–SCORPIO (OCT. 23–NOV. 21)

You adore elegant objects that represent fine taste and aesthetic beauty, and have the ability to transform your environment into a peaceful haven. Scorpio's resourceful and magnetic personality would just love to bask in the sheer elegance of your domain. Your Scorpio lover may enjoy indulging you with the physical pleasures and emotional passions of life while you adorn him or her with appreciation and adoration. The problem, however, is that you may find your Scorpio partner way more intense than you think anyone should ever need to be. You may be attracted by the Scorpio's charisma and want to understand the mysteries behind the veil, but as you look deeper, you may not like what you see. If your Moon is in a water sign (Cancer, Scorpio, or Pisces), you'll be better equipped to react to the powerful Scorpion's emotions, but if your Moon is in an air sign (Gemini, Libra, or Aquarius), you'd better run for the hills while you still can. You are happiest when everything in your environment is in harmony. Scorpio is happiest when passions are running high. If you're willing to take a journey into the shadowy realms of emotions, you just may find more beauty and magic than you can imagine.

LIBRA-SAGITTARIUS (NOV. 22–DEC. 21)

You enjoy outdoor activities where you can appreciate nature, such as environmental programs, community gardens, and hikes. Actually, you Librans make good city planners or designers who seek to bridge the harmony of the aesthetics of nature with urban life. All this bodes well for a relationship with visionary Sagittarius, who is eager to learn, travel, and trek afar for new opportunities. Your Archer will surely bring the bigger picture into your life, whether it's the need for adventure or the need to think about things in a philosophical or global manner. Together, you can blend your high ideals, crafted with the finer touches of intelligence and grace. One problem that may arise comes from your need for harmony and beauty, whereas your Sagittarius lover will forego such abstract pleasures for the next voyage. Unless your Moon or Mars is in a fire sign, you may not always be ready to pack a bag just because he or she has picked a destination. On a smaller scale, you could create little worlds of diverse possibilities right in your own backyard. With a bit of practical assertiveness on your part and an action plan between the two of you, a wide range of options is available for a progressive, harmonious life together.

LIBRA–CAPRICORN (DEC. 22–JAN. 19)

You're attracted to all things beautiful, and although your Capricorn lover may choose practicality over beauty, there is still common ground between you. Your relationship with a Capricorn can produce an environmental blend of your loveliness and his or her austerity. Your partner will be challenged by your "out-of-this-world" dreamy style, for the goal-oriented Goat is relentless about the need to focus on the responsibilities of daily life. It is not that you are lazy, Libra, but you are just not used to putting your nose to the grindstone like the disciplined Capricorn, and you may feel rather burdened by the harsh expectations of your partner. If, however, Venus is in Virgo or Scorpio in your chart, you might be more understanding of this practical way of living. You need time to dream of the fantasy world that you will build in the future. Your Capricorn partner needs to stick to the fundamental nuts and bolts, and needs to take care of business in the present. If the two of you choose to build your paradise on earth together, you'll need to buckle down to the daily routine of practical work while your mate opens his or her imagination to the importance of beauty in your lives.

LIBRA–AQUARIUS (JAN. 20–FEB. 18)

Because you seek harmony in all aspects of life, you're concerned with relationships in general and naturally take on the role of mediator. You find yourself a fine companion in eccentric Aquarius, who is also concerned with the intellectual quality of relationships. Yet there's a difference. Your Aquarius lover is less interested in romantic relationships than in the relationships between abstract ideas and humanity. Theirs is not a warm and fuzzy love, but a powerful idea that can create an unbreakable bond. Your Aquarius partner inspires originality in your aesthetic tastes, while you can help refine his or her radical opinions and blunt assertions. There's an inherent genius between you two air signs, creating a unique mixture of originality, grace, and intelligence. If you choose to have children together, your offspring may carry a wonderful blend of these potentials. Since both signs tend to be primarily mental rather than physical, the Moon, Mercury, or Mars in earth or fire signs in your charts would help you deal with the practical world. In any case, this is a wonderful pair where the two of you can find just the right balance between freedom and companionship.

LIBRA-PISCES (FEB. 19–MARCH 20)

You love to learn about life and yourself through the perception of the people around you. It's one reason why you're a relationship-oriented person. Yet there's an aloof quality about your approach to people that can dominate your personality if you become too absorbed in indulging your self-awareness. When in a relationship with a compassionate and universally minded Pisces, you may discover an avenue of selflessness that you've not previously explored. Pisces is not so interested in self-evolution as much as the continual evolution of the human race. On the surface this sounds like you have something in common, but more often than not, you two will need other indicators in your charts to create compatibility. If the Moon or Venus in your chart is in a water sign, then the emotional underpinning of your Fish won't seem so mysterious and difficult to understand. If the two of you are to prosper as a pair, you'll need to find an acceptable balance between working on achieving harmony in your own relationship and your humanistic concerns. Your innate grace and social skills, coupled with your lover's sensitive nature, can bring about a peaceful resolution to any dissonance you may meet along the path of your relationship.

ABOUT THE AUTHORS

RICK LEVINE   When I first encountered astrology as a psychology undergraduate in the late 1960s, I became fascinated with the varieties of human experience. Even now, I love the one-on-one work of seeing clients and looking at their lives through the cosmic lens. But I also love history and utilize astrology to better under-stand the longer-term cycles of cultural change. My recent DVD, *Quantum Astrology*, explores some of these transpersonal interests. As a scientist, I'm always looking for patterns in order to improve my ability to predict the outcome of any experiment; as an artist, I'm entranced by the mystery of what we do not and cannot know. As an astrologer, I am privileged to live in an enchanted world that links the rational and magical, physical and spiritual—and yes—even science and art.

JEFF JAWER   I'm a Taurus with a Scorpio Moon and Aries rising who lives in the Pacific Northwest with Danick, my double-Pisces musician wife, our two Leo daughters, a black Gemini cat, and a white Pisces dog. I have been a professional astrologer since 1973 when I was a student at the University of Massachusetts (Amherst). I encountered astrology as my first marriage was ending and I was searching for answers. Astrology provided them. More than thirty-five years later, it remains the creative passion of my life as I continue to counsel, write, study, and share ideas with clients and colleagues around the world.

ACKNOWLEDGMENTS

♎

Thanks to Paul O'Brien, our agent, our friend, and the
creative genius behind Tarot.com; Gail Goldberg,
the editor who always makes us sound better; Marcus
Leaver and Michael Fragnito at Sterling Publishing, for
their tireless support for the project; Barbara Berger,
our supervising editor, who has shepherded this book
with Taurean persistence and Aquarian invention; Laura
Jorstad, for her refinement of the text; and Sterling
project editor Mary Hern, editorial assistant Melanie
Madden, and designer Gavin Motnyk for their invaluable
help. We thank Bob Wietrak and Jules Herbert at
Barnes & Noble, and all of the helping hands at Sterling.
Thanks for the art and ideas from Jessica Abel and the
rest of the Tarot.com team. Thanks as well to 3+Co.
for the original design and to Tara Gimmer for the
author photo.

CAMP MENUNKECHOGUE REUNION!!!!!!
HI, GUYS!!!
WELCOME ABOARD. WEAR YOUR T-SHIRTS.
COME ONE**COME ALL!!!**
MAYFLOWER ROOM 2ND FLOOR
LOTS OF GOOD GAMES AND ACTIVITIES PLANNED!!!!!

Nobody will come, thought Vi. Only little kids. Eight-year-olds. I didn't hear from anybody because nobody else would lower themselves. If they're going to the wedding, they'll show up at eight tonight, not for Charles's little games and fun activities.

I was the only one stupid enough to come.

Other Bantam Starfire Books you will enjoy

IN LANE THREE, ALEX ARCHER by Tessa Duder
LOOKS AREN'T EVERYTHING by J. D. Landis
SOMEWHERE BETWEEN LIFE AND DEATH by Lurlene
  McDaniel
TIME TO LET GO by Lurlene McDaniel
A BEGONIA FOR MISS APPLEBAUM by Paul Zindel
FRED SAVAGE: TOTALLY AWESOME by Grace Catalano
AN ALMOST PERFECT SUMMER by Rona S. Zable
DEFINITELY NOT SEXY by Jane Sutton

CAMP REUNION

—

CAROLINE B. COONEY

BANTAM BOOKS
NEW YORK · TORONTO · LONDON · SYDNEY · AUCKLAND

RL 6, Il age 12 and up

CAMP REUNION

A Bantam Starfire Book/November 1988

The Starfire logo is a registered trademark of Bantam Books, a division of Bantam Doubleday Dell Publishing Group, Inc. Registered in U.S. Patent and Trademark Office and elsewhere.

ISBN 0-553-27551-8

Published simultaneously in the United States and Canada

PRINTED IN THE UNITED STATES OF AMERICA

O   0 9 8 7 6 5 4 3

CAMP REUNION

1

Violet wanted to go to the camp reunion so much that every morning she marked off a square on her calendar so she could watch the approach of the great day. And every day she changed her mind and decided not to go. It had been a great summer, much to her surprise. Her campers had adored her, and she'd found a fabulous boyfriend at camp. The idea of a reunion sounded cozy and crowded and huggy: people crying, "Vi! I'm so glad to see you!"; people giving her bear hugs, saying, "Why didn't you write? You were the only one I really wanted to hear from!"

But what if it turned out to be the kind of reunion where people were only glad to see other people, and not her? What if the hugs and kisses steered around her, and she was abandoned in the middle of a huge, barren hotel lobby, with nobody who even remembered her from last summer?

And she would have to talk to her now ex-boyfriend, Jamie, in public. Everybody would be watching. Jamie would be bored. She would be in agony.

Vi and Jamie had conducted a very public romance. What choice had there been? The privacy of camp is zero. No clump of evergreens, no shadow behind the dining hall, no woodsy trail was safe from little spies. Her camper Claudia had actually kept a tally of known kisses. "Let's see," Claudia would say, tapping a pencil against her teeth. "We've got four kisses that Marissa's cabin witnessed. Two kisses Janey watched, and—"

Every week last summer, Vi had gotten one night off. Charles, the camp manager, reluctantly changed Jamie's schedule to permit Jamie to have the same night off. (By the time Charles had agreed to this, there had been only four nights off left in the summer.) When Violet got back from her dates, no matter how late it was, no matter how exhausted her campers should have been from a day of camping, hiking, swimming, canoeing, and dancing, her entire cabin had been waiting up.

They had wanted details.

"Nothing romantic," they would tell Vi firmly. They could read about romance in books. From her they wanted anatomical material. "But what was the kiss like?" they would demand. "What exactly did he do? And for how many seconds? And what did you do? Show us what your face looked like then. Did your hair get in your eyes?"

Vi could just imagine the reunion: Claudia with her kiss book open, and a dozen little girls gig-

2

gling, while Vi had to admit out loud that Jamie had never called her after the summer was over.

The fantasies her cabin had come up with! Jamie and Vi would date forever, the girls decided, and have children, and tell the children how their parents had fallen in love at Camp Girl-Meets-Boy. (Everybody shortened Camp Menunkechogue to Camp Men, but Vi had carried it a step further. "It's Camp Girl-Meets-Boy," she'd explained to her campers. "And I came to Camp Men to meet the perfect boy.")

But the moment he drove out the camp gate, Jamie forgot Vi. Vi had wept more nights than she cared to remember. What if she cried at the reunion? What if Jamie sauntered up (in the formal clothing she had hardly ever seen on him, because at camp Jamie prided himself on being clothed only from the waist down) and she burst into tears? She who had kissed and loved him—was she supposed to shake hands? Ask after his mother? Offer him a stick of gum?

Better to sit home that terrifying Saturday, alone, with a mirror and depression.

Violet's mother was exasperated with all this. "Honey, there will be hundreds of people there. And I promise you, not a single one will care whether Jamie asked you out after the summer ended."

Was this supposed to be comforting?

What good was life if people didn't care what Violet was doing?

Her mother's attempts to comfort Vi hardly ever worked. Vi's mother felt humans were paltry stars

3

in a vast Milky Way. Vi preferred to think of herself as the sun, with everybody else revolving around her.

"Mother," said Vi, getting down to essentials, "I'll need a new dress."

"Violet, it's a camp reunion. You don't need a new dress, you need an old T-shirt."

Violet counted the calendar days left. Very few for a major shopping expedition. She flung open closet doors and bureau drawers to prove how inadequate her wardrobe was. "Mother, it is not simply a camp reunion. It's also, as you well know, Charles and Alicia's wedding."

They were in Vi's room surrounded by half-open drawers. School for Vi and work for her mother were over for the day. Vi peeled off her wool pants and extra long L. L. Bean shirt, while her mother got out of her hospital uniform. Around the house they both preferred sweat suits.

"I think that is idiotic," said Vi's mother, now down to pale green lace bra and panties. "What kind of people would have a combination camp reunion and wedding? Alicia's family clearly has no sense of etiquette."

Vi flicked her sweatpants at the wall with irritation. "Mother!" They were at a stage where it was difficult to chat for sixty seconds without confrontation. "It is *not* a combination reunion and wedding. They're not going to mix the camp pledge with the wedding vows. It's just that there's a camp reunion planned for the Saturday after Thanksgiving anyway, and since Charles and Alicia want the same people to be at their wedding, it's logical to

4

have the reunion in the afternoon and the wedding in the evening."

Now they were both in nothing but bra and panties. They glared at each other, like sumo wrestlers. "I don't think it's logical at all," said her mother. "I think it's queer."

Vi stalked into the bathroom and looked in the mirror, mentally dressing herself in a wedding gown.

Of course, Alicia was marrying Charles. That was a silly decision. Vi had no use for Charles whatsoever. The fact that it was Charles that Alicia would meet at the altar did dampen Vi's enthusiasm for the whole thing. Still—a wedding. Who could dislike weddings? And it was so romantic that the camp nurse had fallen in love with the camp owner/manager.

Vi's mother began poking through Vi's sweat-shirt collection. She'll stretch them, thought Vi, but said nothing.

"I detest weddings," said her mother, stretching the Ski Vermont sweatshirt. "You know they're going to get divorced in a year, anyhow, and you've wasted all that money on a gift."

"They are not going to get divorced!" shouted Vi. Although she personally would have a marriage to Charles annulled by midnight. Charles was very suspicious of Vi. He thought that any girl who brought hot rollers and a lighted makeup mirror to a Maine wilderness camp was bound to cause trouble. ("If you leave those appliances of yours plugged in, Violet," Charles had yelled at her once, "and your cabin catches fire, and the forest catches fire, and all the innocent furry little animals . . ."

"I am not going to murder anybody, Charles!" Vi had screamed back. "I'm just going to have curly hair, all right?")

She and Charles had never reached friendship. Or even armed truce. Vi had been invited to the wedding because of Alicia. Violet decided to sit on Alicia's side of the church, or hotel as the case was here, and possibly make a face at Charles when nobody was looking.

"Why are you always talking divorce these days, Mother?" demanded Violet. "It's not very romantic. Not everybody in the whole world is getting divorced."

"Sure feels like it," her mother muttered.

This was because Vi's older sister, Jasmine, had just abandoned her husband of two years to come back home and live. There was no real reason, as Jasmine was the first to admit. Her husband was not a drunk, a druggie, or a violent man. He earned money regularly and took out the garbage and cooked on alternate nights. "I was bored," said Jasmine.

"You promised to love, honor, and cherish that man till death do you part," screamed her parents. "And we gave you the most splendid wedding we could afford—in fact, more than we could afford— and you abandon him *because you're bored*?"

Vi's older sister said that, if all her mother and father cared about was the money, and not their daughter's happiness, then she was very disappointed in their values.

"*Our* values!" screamed the parents.

And so on, and so forth, night after night, until in that household, the very word wedding was enough to make people draw their weapons. Violet decided not to start yet another argument about weddings. She needed the whole evening to consider what her wedding gift was going to be, anyhow.

Still, the problem of what to wear loomed large. Vi kept waiting for the appropriate minute to reinforce the idea that she needed a new dress, but there never was such a moment. Finally she went to her grandmother. This was a strategical error, because Grandma was even more upset over Jasmine than anybody, and practically had a heart attack when Vi mentioned weddings.

That's all I need, thought Vi, fixing her grandmother tea and cookies. Grandma having cardiac arrest at my feet because I ask for a dress. Then Mother and Dad will *really* know their two daughters have sick values.

In the end, Violet went to Jasmine. "Listen," she said to her sister. "You've wrecked my family life and I'm forgiving you only if you buy me a dress."

This appealed to Jasmine, not because she worried about Vi's family life, but because shopping was her favorite activity. Jasmine knew every size-eight rack from the local mall to San Francisco. Jasmine leaped into the project with enthusiasm. (Jasmine loved weddings; in fact she hoped to have a second of her own, one of these days.) So Vi ended up with a new reunion outfit (which also looked good on Jasmine) *and* a new wedding outfit

7

(which looked excellent on Jasmine), because Jasmine understood these were not the same event and a person could not appear badly dressed at either one, not when important things like Jamie were at stake. Jasmine even loaned Vi a sexy, silken gown and peignoir that had been a shower gift to Jasmine.

Vi felt like a bride herself in the shimmering folds of ivory lace and silk. Would the other girls sharing the hotel suite ever be impressed now!

But thinking of those girls made Vi quiver. For it was not really Jamie who worried her most. It was Marissa.

Marissa and Vi had shared responsibility for the twelve-year-old girl campers. They were cool with each other at first. Marissa was the kind of camp counselor who could identify constellations and paw prints and leaves, while Vi was the kind who was good at hair conditioners. Marissa loved how the cabins were nestled in the forest, while Violet felt that every crackling twig probably meant Big Foot come to kill her. Vi brought so much clothing and makeup, she needed help towing it up the cliff path to her cabin, while Marissa brought so little you would have thought she was staying half an hour, not ten weeks.

Summer had passed.

Vi struggled with campers who wet the bed and insisted on playing the trumpet when they were not musical, and who, instead of sleeping through the night like normal people, were always having M&M's fights at two in the morning, or pretending to be rats at three in the morning.

8

Marissa's cabin always won inspection, and swam like dolphins, and knew the middle verses to all the camp songs. Vi's cabin was always late for supper because they were practicing using her eye shadow.

Slowly, reluctantly, Vi and Marissa had become friends. By the end of summer they were inseparable friends. They could talk about everything. Whether Sinclair ("Call me Sin") Franklin would ever love Marissa the way Marissa loved Sin. Whether Cathy deserved to be shot, or if Charles should be pushed off a cliff. The last day of camp, they had wept saying good-bye, and promised to be friends forever.

But Marissa had never telephoned Vi. Never written. And something—what?—had held Vi back, too. Perhaps they had not been friends at all, and the closeness that had developed between them over July and August was only a truce. Perhaps when Marissa returned to her own high school and her own friends, Vi had paled in comparison and Marissa forgot her.

Vi knew now about summer romances.

She had not known there could be summer friends.

Oh, what if nobody at the reunion remembered her?

What if Marissa said vaguely, "Oh, hi—uh—let's see—it's . . ."

What if Jamie was hugging somebody else when Vi got there?

What if Cathy said in her cruel way, "I think it's Violet. Were you Violet?"

9

I won't go, thought Vi. Better to miss the whole reunion than risk that.

"Yes, you will too go," said Jasmine. "If you think I bought you all that stuff and you're not wearing it, you're wrong. You're going."

2

Cathy Coatsworth was breathtakingly beautiful.

Her looks could quiet a room. Her boyfriend, Channing, had called her his golden dove. Channing, who'd been in college, seemed never to worry about classes or papers. He was handsome in the smooth sort of way that would have given him the role of European royal lover if they had starred together in a movie.

Cathy used to love to appear in public with Channing. When she and Channing drifted into a room, motion and conversation stopped, while everybody paused to pay homage to their beauty.

Channing had had friends everywhere. She and Channing always had somebody to meet, and her social schedule was crammed beyond belief. She loved boasting about it. She could think of no teenage girl whose life was so busy.

Last summer, when Channing had told Cathy he had to make a few trips to South America, she'd loved hearing that. He was only twenty, yet he sounded like an oil tycoon or a diplomat. But she hadn't known what to do with herself. Her parents were going to Europe, and her older brother and sister were busy, too. She hadn't wanted to be home, hanging around alone. And she hadn't wanted to go to Europe with her parents. Finally, she'd decided to be a dance counselor at an overnight camp. She'd loved the idea of being worshipped by hundreds of little girls, who would all want to grow up to be exactly like her.

When September came, Channing thought it was hysterically funny that Cathy, of all people, the golden dove, had been a camp counselor. Cathy was an excellent storyteller. She routinely had people's eyes on her, but after her summer camp experience, she told funny stories and captured their ears, too. "Well, there was Marissa, pitiful thing," Cathy would begin, gluing the audience to herself. "Or was her name Melissa? She didn't have much personality. She was always off rejoicing in the scent of hemlocks on the nature trail. Marissa's idea of a big day was making fern bookmarks in arts and crafts."

They would be in a disco or a new place to eat, and Cathy would reinvent her camp stories to get an easy laugh. "You should have heard all these kids saying their little pledge," Cathy would mock, placing her manicured nails on her heart! "They were so serious. *I promise to show the world I am a Camp Menunkechogue girl*."

"Camp what?" Everybody would giggle.

"Camp Menunkechogue," Cathy would say, in her fluttery dovelike coo. "Rhymes with *Go catch a hog*, or *Let's breathe some smog*." This always brought more laughs, but Cathy had never given credit to Violet, whose rhymes they were.

"Was Cathy really a counselor at this camp, Channing?" somebody would demand, laughing.

Cathy would preen before them, her green eyes glittering, her ivory complexion and shimmering hair and perfect figure all glowing.

"A brief lapse in intelligence," Channing would agree.

Cathy would start everybody laughing, but the beautiful couple never stayed long. Cathy loved the way Channing always left a room swiftly, while he and she were still the center of attention, as if they were far too busy to spend more than a few minutes in any one place.

Until October twenty-third.

On October twenty-third, Cathy Coatsworth had found herself in a police station. Her parents were there, and her brother and sister, and a lawyer.

Cathy was not speaking because she could not stop sobbing. Her family was not speaking because they were so shocked. The lawyer was not speaking because he felt silence was safer.

Cathy's family could not even look at Cathy. Their daughter? Their sister? Mixed up in drug deals?

"But I wasn't," said Cathy despairingly. "I didn't even know. I was just—just there."

13

The police, of course, stared at Cathy. The way men and boys always stared at Cathy. They took in the hair, golden as shining sunsets. They stared at the lovely voluptuous figure, the perfect tan, the huge brilliant green eyes. The perfect face, white teeth, sexy smile, and sensuous walk.

Cathy thought, they're not looking at me, Cathy Coatsworth. They're looking at the parts: like options on an expensive car. *Hey, look at it shine. I wouldn't mind polishing that one.*

Channing, however, had had plenty to say. It was as if, having been caught, he now found it necessary to produce details so that he would be admired for brilliance of planning. Channing's lawyer also advised silence, but Channing had never been able to bear silence.

"And what about Miss Coatsworth?" a police officer had asked Channing.

Cathy had never been referred to as Miss Coatsworth. It sounded as if she had become scum, and the officer had to distance himself from her. She would never again be called Cathy, because it was too affectionate.

"Who cares about her?" said Channing to the officer. "I only had her there because she's so gorgeous. People stare. Men leer. And Cathy is the most conceited girl on earth. She's always playing to an audience. If people don't stare, then she knocks herself out until they do. All Cathy was was good camouflage."

Cathy had reached for a chair, trying to sit before her body turned to jelly and she disgraced herself. But there were no chairs, and nobody offered to get

14

her one. They merely looked at her in contempt. Her own parents. Her own brother. Her own sister. Their faces were identical, as if the curled lip and disgusted frown were drawn by the same cartoonist.

Channing added, "So, while they soaked up Cathy, I'd do the drug deal. She's not an accessory crimewise. She was an accessory like a piece of jewelry is. I'd just hang her out front and nobody would notice what I was doing." Channing laughed. "Especially Cathy wouldn't notice. She only notices herself, anyway."

Channing's contempt was even greater than that of her family, or the police. For Channing—whom she had adored—Cathy had been a float in a parade. All that wonderful social life: those people had been buyers, and she had been there to distract attention, so that strangers would not notice Channing's deals in the filth.

October twenty-third.

Her involvement with the police had not been for much more than just that one day. Channing had been so ready to talk that the police limited their interrogation of Cathy. They came a couple of times to the house, but she could add nothing to what they'd already learned. For Channing was right; she had noticed only herself, and never the people to whom she played.

It's one thing to know you've done something wrong. To see that your attractive little personality has a smudge.

It's quite another to know that you're the wrong kind of person altogether: that you're nothing but one big smudge.

Cathy's parents were not speaking to her.

Cathy's older sister was not speaking to her.

Cathy's younger brother and grandparents were not speaking to her.

I'm not even speaking to myself, thought Cathy.

It was true. She fixed her mind on things like which shoes to wear: the dark gray flats with the tiny black ribbon woven through the leather, or the lighter gray shoes with the more rounded toe. Cathy found if you tried hard enough, you could skip thinking altogether.

You couldn't escape at night, though.

There was something about the darkness that brought dreadful thoughts like little toads hopping onto the bed with you, their nasty warty green fingers gripping your skin, peeling it back, oozing into your brain.

Cathy slept with the lights on.

It was now November twenty-first, and Cathy had not yet figured out how to dress, or do her hair, or even walk.

Every time she flung back her hair—the thick golden glistening hair she was so proud of—she thought of Channing using that pose. Every time she pulled jeans over her long slim legs she thought of how she used to walk. Slowly, teasingly, trying to get the most attention from the most members of the opposite sex.

I'm not a person, thought Cathy. I'm an accessory.

She couldn't quite throw away her actual accessories, but she couldn't look at them, either. Not ust the word, but also the ornaments offended her. She packed them all away in boxes: the belts, the earrings, the scarves, the purse collection, the sunglasses in all shades and shapes. Without them, the bedroom was bare and temporary. She felt bare when she left the house. She who had always cared so intensely about fashion and figure and face now appeared only as a stripped-down model.

A car without accessories, Cathy thought. You see me here, nothing but four wheels and an engine. No radio, no air conditioning, no speed control.

She could hardly fill her time anymore. When you didn't spend the evening planning what to wear the next day, and spend the next day shopping for what to wear the following day, what did you do? When you used to spend a happy hour trying on different belts and sashes and scarves and socks—and now you were the stripped-down model—what happened during that hour?

Nothing that Cathy could find.

She was not bored, exactly. She was stunned. Vacant. But it was not surprising to be vacant.

Men still stared at her. In a way it was gratifying. It proved she certainly did not need the accessories to be beautiful and appealing. But it proved something else, something terrible. She herself would always be just an accessory.

Then the invitation to the camp reunion arrived.

She had read it and folded it and wrinkled it up by spindling it with her fingernails (nails with no polish for the first time since she was eleven.) It always said the same thing, announced in big cheery script. Camp Menunkechogue had a reunion every five years and all former camp counselors and campers were welcome to come to the Hilton on the afternoon of Saturday, November twenty-ninth.

They have my name down on their mailing list only because Charles wrote a computer program and forgot to take me off, thought Cathy. I'm not really welcome. Nobody liked me. I was mean to Marissa. I called her Melissa on purpose. And when Marissa got all earnest, at her most camp counselor-y, I'd coo to the boys, "Isn't she cute?" I could always make them laugh at Marissa. I could even make Sin laugh at her—when I knew she had a crush on him. . . . And Violet. Little, fluffy, dopey Vi. I was furious when Jamie fell for her. . . . And of course I couldn't be bothered to make the effort to learn the little campers' names. I would write to Channing and call them "the campies." It didn't bother me at all to mix up JoAnne and Roxanne . . . but I bet it bothered JoAnne and Roxanne.

Cathy tortured herself by the hour about her behavior at camp. Once she even got out her Camp Men T-shirt and wore it around the house, to remind herself that she was probably the least kind counselor any little girl in Maine ever suffered.

I want to be like Marissa, thought Cathy. Or even like Vi.

It seemed to Cathy that Marissa and Vi were from another era: a better, finer time, where personalities were unstained and kindness was unending.

One of Vi's campers had wet the bed. Cathy could not even bear to be near Laury, it was so disgusting that a twelve-year-old girl would do that. Vi had never once referred to it. Not in front of little Laury, not in front of the rest of the campers. Vi had just held her breath and dragged Laury's mattress outside to air. Laury had worshipped Vi. Cathy, as dance instructor, had wanted all the little girls to worship *her*. She'd resented Laury's dumb adoration of dumb old Violet.

I was jealous of a little girl's love, thought Cathy, wishing that she, like Channing, were facing a jail sentence. At least if you went to jail, you paid your debt to society. How was she ever going to pay her debt to Laury?

Cathy shuddered remembering the time when, during a dance practice, she had made Laury dance alone in front of twenty other girls. And then Cathy had said cruelly, "Laury, what is this perfume you're treating us to? My dear, you smell like an outhouse." Laury had frozen middance, mouth open, ankle dangling. Cathy had taunted her, "Can you last through the dance, Laury?" Laury had hunched down, trying to grow younger and smaller. And Cathy had laughed at her. Cathy had an infectious laugh; she was proud of her laugh. Cathy's laugh had leadership—when Cathy laughed, people joined in.

So all twenty girls had laughed at Laury.

Cathy tried to remember the last time she had been nice. It was a long time ago: elementary school. There was a girl named Monnie, and Cathy let Monnie sit next to her even though Monnie was a dope.

That was me at my best, thought Cathy, sobbing in her room. *Letting* a girl sit next to me. The *honor* of sitting next to me was me being nice.

Cathy had been invited to the reunion. She could go, just like anybody else.

It was being held at the Hilton, a huge, anonymous, splashy hotel. If the reunion was too terrible, she could always vanish into another dining room or another meeting room, or even take a taxi and come home early.

If it were wonderful however . . .

That was ridiculous. It could not be wonderful. Cathy doubted that anything in her life would be wonderful again. She was not a good person. Why would Vi and Marissa even speak to her?

Cathy dried her tears with her Camp Men T-shirt.

Oh, they'd speak to her all right.

Vi and Marissa were courteous. And they'd remember their little Camp Men pledge, the one Cathy had considered too silly to repeat at flag-lowering ceremonies by the lake. *I promise to be a friend to people around me and to the earth. I promise to love the world and all her glories. I promise to encourage, to praise, and to be patient. To let the world know I am a Camp Menunkechogue girl.*

Cathy wet her lips, and the creased invitation she held in her hand quivered. It seemed to her that if she could spend even one afternoon with good people, she could catch hold of their goodness. Even a straw, a splinter, of goodness would be better than this nothingness that gripped her now. Maybe some of the terrible warty green toads of the night would leave her alone if she could just see Marissa and Vi, and memorize them, and imitate them.

3

———

Claudia did not reply to the invitation even though it had included an RSVP.

She knew this was bad manners, but how were you supposed to make up your mind on that sort of thing until the very last minute? Claudia felt you should be able to RSVP at the door.

For the first eleven years, Claudia's life was perfect. She had not really noticed her life; she just sailed along enjoying everything from spelling to blue jeans, from her cousins to her haircuts.

And then Daddy—perfect Daddy—came home to say he was tired of being married to Mommy and was going to marry Heather Anne. Claudia would always remember how her parents ceased to be Mommy and Daddy that afternoon, and by nightfall, had become Mommy and "him." Neither Claudia nor her mother could bring themselves to use the word *Daddy* at all, so they rearranged their sentences. *"He* says . . ." *"He* lied again . . ." "Did you talk to *him*?"

And then Daddy's partner at work, Jonathan, was suddenly comforting Mommy quite a lot. Jonathan and Mommy had taken Claudia out to dinner once, both of them giggling. There was something disgusting and untrustworthy about grown-ups giggling. And sure enough, sitting by candlelight at the Chateau Rose, Mommy leaned over the plates of salad—Claudia was busy picking out the inedible parts, like mushrooms—and said it was all for the best, wasn't it, Claudia, darling? Every cloud had a silver lining and things worked out in the end, because Mommy was going to marry Jonathan now and they would all live happily ever after.

Claudia certainly doubted *that* conclusion.

Now there were two men Claudia could not call by name, and now the sentences really got complex, and required a lot of hand gestures so that the listener could guess which "he" was being referred to—her father or Jonathan.

She staggered through the winter of sixth grade. Teachers still gave arithmetic quizzes, and pencils still got blunt; she still sang soprano in the spring concert, and the Memorial Day parade arrived right on time.

About then had come the announcement that Claudia was to spend the whole summer at some wilderness camp in Maine. She could not believe ey were serious. Bugs and creepy noises? Wet feet on cold days? Nasty strange girls singing stupid songs?

24

Summer was the good time. She would swim at the country club, play tennis with her girlfriends, ride her bike all over, and swing in the hammock, reading good books. (Bad books she would hurl across the lawn like Frisbees, which made returning them to the library tricky, but now that Jonathan had taken over library fines, Claudia liked to run them up wherever possible.)

Summer was a time to daydream and wander in hot long days, where the hours stretched, your tan deepened, and your friends waited for you on the porch.

"Camp?" Claudia had said. "What—are you kidding me?"

It seemed that this was Heather Anne's first marriage, and of course she had a right to a huge splashy wedding, which could not possibly be put together before September and would take up ever so much time. Claudia would be happier out of the way.

It seemed that Jonathan and Mommy also wanted a large wedding, and this, too, would take weeks to plan, and Claudia would be happier out of their way as well.

"What you're saying is, you guys want to ship me off so you can have fun," accused Claudia.

Of course not, said the four grown-ups, wherever did you get such an idea?

Heather Anne cajoled her to behave by showing her the lovely pale lavender satin gown Claudia would wear at their wedding. Claudia said purple was a low-class color and nobody with taste would choose that for a wedding.

Mommy and Jonathan told her she could pick her own color gown for their wedding. Claudia said she would wear black, to symbolize the mourning she would be in for her real family.

"I'll write to you all summer long," promised her mother.

"I won't write back," promised Claudia.

"Now, Claudia," said her father, "why can't you behave sensibly?"

Sensible meant that she should make things easy for them. Well, Claudia hated them all, and she could not believe she had to go to this Camp Menunke-something that you couldn't even pronounce, with all the weirdo mill-nerds that would undoubtedly like such a dump.

"What's a mill-nerd?" her father had asked.

"A nerd times a million," said Claudia. "Like you."

But when they arrived at camp, having driven past a billion pine trees to get there, Claudia's rage collapsed. She was afraid and desperate. They would go and get married and start new homes and leave her here because she'd been so mean to them, and she would never again have even half a family.

Her father and Heather Anne drove away. Claudia was left in the clutches of a counselor named Violet, who bore a sickening resemblance to Heather Anne: all fluff and yellow. But when Vi hauled her up a path so steep that Claudia said they should install chair lifts, Vi laughed so hard she almost fell off the cliff. In the tiny brown-shingled cabin were eight bunks; narrow hard bunks on which you unrolled your sleeping bag and stuck your pillow. Vi had brought designer sheets and monogrammed pink cotton blankets. Claudia met Janey and Laury right away and the three girls had sat cross-legged on Vi's designer sheets and Vi had taught them how to apply liquid eyeliner and then they had all done their nails and Claudia chose purple with gold flecks. By supper they were best friends.

Claudia could not get over how quickly you made friends at camp. Back home she'd had lots of friends, but they hadn't meant as much. The intimacy of eight girls and a crazy counselor in one tiny room, overflowing with sneakers, teddy bears, wet bathing suits, postcards from home, cassettes, nature notebooks, and crafts projects had been a wonderful thing.

Claudia had never written home. Each week you had to submit a letter before supper to show you were communicating, and Claudia had mailed empty envelopes. Vi had never told on her, and at least her parents knew she was alive, because the envelopes had been addressed in Claudia's handwriting.

The summer was wonderful.

How excruciatingly painful it had been to say good-bye to her cabinmates, her fellow campers, and Vi and Marissa. She hurt all over, and had wept in the car as they drove through Maine, and reached Massachusetts, and hurtled down the Connecticut Turnpike toward home.

In one week, school started.

A week after that, her father and Heather Anne

married, and Claudia was a bridesmaid in pale lavender satin.

Three weeks later, her mother and Jonathan married, and Claudia was a bridesmaid in lemon yellow.

It had been like having convulsions. Claudia's body jerked from one huge event to another. Claudia forgot camp. It vanished as if it had never been.

In the midst of all this came her thirteenth birthday. The four adults had gotten together in civilized terms to throw her an enormous party. They invited everybody Claudia had ever spoken to. Along with cake and favors and barbecue, there was a clown, a magician, a band, and a tethered hot-air balloon so everybody could take safe little rides. Everybody said it was the best birthday party they had ever come to.

The only thing Claudia could say about it was that she sure felt older. Thirteen was immeasurably older than twelve. At twelve you still thought wishes and tantrums could change the course of events.

Junior high was good because it was big. Five elementary schools fed into it, and Claudia was absorbed into the fabric of junior high—just another thread. But her two new families . . . she was not part of either one. School was safe. Home was sad.

When the invitation to the camp reunion arrived, Claudia was spending the weekend with her father and Heather Anne. Claudia did not enjoy

28

weekends with them. But it was worse staying with Mommy and Jonathan, who loved being by themselves, and whose faces would crumple in disappointment if Claudia said the awful words, "I'm staying with you."

The four grown-ups had asked her opinion, of course, before setting up the stay-with-which-parent-when arrangement. They didn't want to leave her out of anything, they explained. Claudia informed them that they had left her totally out of the only thing she wanted (her original family), and that they could set up any goddamn schedule they wanted.

Never had Claudia uttered a swear word to her parents, and only a half dozen times in her life had she said the word at all. The four parents told each other it was junior high, having a bad influence on her; seventh-graders were known for their un-civilized behavior.

"It's you," cried Claudia, "who are uncivilized. What about your marriage vows, Mommy? What about yours, Daddy? Broken, all of them. I call that uncivilized. What example do you think *you* are setting?"

Claudia became expert at this. Her timing was good, too. She didn't toss off these remarks when people were busy doing the dishes or figuring their income tax. She made sure there were other adults around to increase the embarrassment, to make her parents pay.

Once her mother broke down. "Don't you care if I'm happy or not?" she wept.

"No," said Claudia, quite surprised that her mother had not yet caught on.

Claudia fingered the invitation. Printed on a computer with advanced graphics. Charles was in love with computers. Claudia leaned back against the pillows piled on this bed (all her friends told her that at least she got two bedrooms out of the remarriages; Claudia didn't see what the big deal was in that; all it meant was that anything you wanted was always in the other house).

She examined the invitation only to find a second one tucked inside—to the wedding of Charles and Alicia! Claudia was amazed. She did not have a high opinion of weddings and she was sorry that anyone as terrific as Alicia, the camp nurse, was having one.

From the kitchen her stepmother's high airy voice floated. "Claudia, dear! Claudia, honey!"

Claudia stuck her invitations under the pillows. She was certainly not going to risk sharing them with Heather Anne.

"Dinner!" called Heather Anne. "Wash your hands!"

I'm a baby? thought Claudia. Or a disgusting dweeb of a junior-high boy? I have to be *told* to be clean?

Claudia washed ferociously, turning her hands pruney, splashing water and soap all over her bathroom and leaving the wet towel on the floor. She entered the dining room like a messenger entering the enemy camp. It was definitely Heather Anne's room. White lace hung over a deep pink tablecloth. Pink scented candles in silver

30

sticks had been lit. The roses her father had brought Heather Anne yesterday were still fresh in their crystal vase. The room was one, big, pink, silver, and crystal wedding-present collection.

Claudia ignored everything her father and Heather Anne said to her. She thought of Alicia. Last summer, Alicia had taped Claudia's sprained ankle, and rubbed soothing medication into her sunburn, and was the only person who was kind when, on a camping trip, Claudia went into the trees to go to the bathroom, and picked leaves for paper and the leaves turned out to be poison ivy. "You are the only girl in the history of Camp Men with carnal knowledge of poison ivy," said Alicia, comforting Claudia in her itchy agony. "What's carnal knowledge?" Claudia had said, and Alicia, being a nurse, gave the most intensive sex education lecture Claudia was ever to receive in her life.

Claudia had known what sex was, of course, but not quite so graphically, not with such a wealth of detail. It was really disgusting to picture Daddy and Heather Anne, or Mommy and Jonathan doing that. It made you positively prefer poison ivy.

At the dinner table Claudia thought, Ick. Alicia is going to do that with Charles? Ick. And Charles is so old!

Heather Anne had made coleslaw. Claudia hated mayonnaise and hated cabbage and had told Heather Anne a hundred times. And the steak was rare. Practically bloody. Claudia felt sick ev looking at raw meat.

Back when her *real* family existed, there had

been no Heather Anne to serve disgusting food. But it was no use changing houses. Claudia's own mother no longer served good, comforting, dull stuff. Like Kraft Macaroni and Cheese, or instant mashed potatoes. "Jonathan doesn't like that," Mommy would say, serving some horrid crunchy thing with wormy-looking Japanese vegetables.

It seemed to Claudia that the last good thing in her life was Camp Menunkechogue and the last two people who truly loved her were her counselor, Vi, and her camp nurse, Alicia.

"Now, Claudia," said her father. "Some dear old friends of Heather Anne's are going to be in town the weekend of November twenty-ninth. The Saturday after Thanksgiving. That's your weekend with us, but you can stay with Mommy and Jonathan, can't you." He put no question mark in his sentence. He was telling her.

"Why?" said Claudia. "You don't want to introduce me to Heather Anne's dear old friends?"

"Claudia, don't be rude."

You're the rude ones, thought Claudia. Always shipping me off. A few months ago she would have screamed at them. Tonight she let it pass. She had another roll, since there was nothing else edible. Wait. The Saturday after Thanksgiving Mommy and Jonathan were having a big cocktail party, which they had planned for that date because she was to be here, with Daddy and Heather Anne. "Oh—but—"

"But what?" said Heather Anne.

"Nothing." Claudia finished her roll. Nobody

wants me, she thought. Some Thanksgiving it will be. Two days later I'm an abandoned kid.

Heather Anne yelled at her for not eating any protein. Her father yelled at her for not cooperating. Claudia didn't cry, didn't break the wedding presents or start a food fight. She went back up to her room and stared at her homework. It blurred before her eyes. She leaned against the pillows and heard something crunch. She fished the reunion invitation out, smoothed away the wrinkles and reread it. It was also for the Saturday after Thanksgiving.

I'll just go, thought Claudia. Why tell anybody? I won't be at anybody's house, and I bet none of them will even notice. I'll spend the night with somebody they've never even heard of, and maybe I won't even come back at all.

So there.

4

Marissa had a date for the wedding.

Normal teenagers went to the movies on their first date. Or to McDonald's for french fries. Or to Friendly's for ice cream. But no, Marissa's first date with Sinclair Franklin was to a wedding.

What would it be like, sitting together while Alicia and Charles took their marriage vows? Would Sin murmur to her, "Boy, you'll never catch me saying that!" Or would he whisper, "Gosh, Mariss—kind of makes you dream, doesn't it?"

Marissa had had a crush on Sin since last spring, when they'd found out they were going to be counselors together at Camp Men. The crush had become a burden, the sort only Sin's wide shoulders could carry, but Sin had no crush at all. He liked Marissa and that was it. They talked easily on the phone now, because they'd both been campers themselves at Camp Men for years and then counselors and so they had a thousand memories in common.

But while Marissa could recall every syllable of every conversation, Sin was more likely to forget he had ever spoken to her, and his side of the conversation was usually a rerun of what he had said the last time.

But this time—this sacred time!—Sin had said on the phone, "Say, Mariss. Want to go to the wedding with me?" Sin's voice was cheerful and rather bouncy. It didn't suit his looks, which were strong and solid. Sin was shaped like a triangle, with extremely wide shoulders, as if he had come into the world prepadded for football, and from there he dwindled into slim waist and narrow hips. Sin's clothes never quite fit because all the fabric needed at the shoulders just dangled around the rest of him.

"Sure," Marissa had said casually, although it was the most exciting invitation of her love life.

"Okay," Sin had said, as if they were ordering groceries. "Now let's match. I'll feel better if we match. What're you wearing?"

"I haven't decided yet."

"I'm wearing a suit," Sin had proclaimed, as if this were so extraordinary he didn't want her to faint when she saw him. "With a vest. It's very dark gray, and you can just barely make out the plaid, because it's so sophisticated, and cream-lored, button-down-collar oxford shirt, and a very dark red tie. I look great."

Marissa was sure of that.

Sin had said, "So you think gray and cream and dark red, Marissa?"

Marissa had assured him she thought this quite often.

When she got off the phone she told her mother, and her mother said, "I suppose you think I'm going to take you shopping until we find a suitable wedding-guest outfit in that color combination? I suppose you think we're just going to ignore that lovely dark blue wool paisley and forget about the skirt and sweater your grandmother got you, and pretend you don't own the striped—" Her mother sighed. Her mother made threatening gestures toward the checkbook and purse. Then she laughed. "Actually, I like Sin, too," she confided. "We'd better get started. What store shall we hit first?"

Gray and cream and dark red ruled their lives. It was the old story: the moment you've decided on a color combination, it goes out of fashion and nobody stocks it.

Marissa and her mother went shopping every day after school and found nothing except dull matronly clothes for which Marissa would have had to gain fifty pounds and dye her hair gray to look right in. "I don't know why we're going through all this torment for Sin," complained her mother. "We could just as easily go through it all for Heath. Why don't you call Heath and see what he's wearing? Maybe you could match him more easily."

All the girls at Camp Men had adored Heath. Dark and romantic, with a family fraught with sad secrets—who could ask for anything more? Heath

Hesper had been an excellent camp counselor. Hurling his intense energy into making camp the perfect place on earth for little boys, Heath had hung on to his sanity. He told nobody about himself, earning from Violet the nickname Dark, as in "I'm in the dark about you, Heath." They all made up stories about Heath. None of them was even remotely right. For it wasn't Heath's story at all that mattered; it was his father's. Heath couldn't even have his own tragedy. He was whipped by somebody else's.

In the last few moments at camp, while everyone was saying their tearful farewells, Heath had said, in their presence, "I'll call you, Marissa." And then he had hugged her, hard, and kissed her, harder.

Naturally everybody drew conclusions from this.

She and Heath would begin dating and her social life would be perfect. Camp was in northern Maine, but home to most of the campers and counselors was in Westchester County and New York City. Marissa had planned joyously for dates: how she would go into Manhattan on the train and have dinner with Heath, and how Heath would come up to Rye to see her, and go to the high-school dances.

It turned out, however, that when Heath had said "call," he'd meant "call." As in phone. He had a hundred problems and he wanted to air them with Marissa. By phone.

His problems were impressive by any standards, including the standards of the *New York Times*, the *Washington Post*, and ABC, NBC, and CBS, but

Marissa was crushed. How she blushed when she remembered her fantasies. And her mother was amused. Marissa hated that more than anything— her mother laughing slightly on Mondays when Heath called. Marissa hated, hated, hated being laughed at.

Mondays were hardest for him: he had the break of the weekend to hibernate in his apartment and pretend that what was happening wasn't. Then when school started, he had to face once more his friends and enemies. His father's trial was getting very heavy media coverage. Headlines said, WALL STREET RIPOFF ARTIST NOW ADMITS TO MORE THAN 20 MIL. And there was HESPER TESTIFIES IT WAS FUN. Another nice one was HESPER FAMILY RICH FOREVER ON TRICK TRADES.

On Mondays Heath would call Marissa to tell her in detail how he was feeling and how rotten it was. She became Heath's safety valve. But I'm just sixteen! thought Marissa. I don't want to be your shrink. I want to be your girlfriend!

Heath didn't want to hold her hand or kiss her lips. She was Clorox to pour on the dirty laundry of his troubles, and maybe he would feel cleaner after he talked to her.

As for the kiss and hug, Marissa knew now that Heath had just been afraid to go home. The protection and the isolation of camp had ended. All that kiss had done was extend his safety zone a minute.

Last Monday when Heath called, Marissa had been lying on the floor of her bedroom with her feet up on the bed, staring at a poster of Billy Idol and thinking that, of her own two idols, Heath and Sin, emotion ran depressingly one way.

Did they idolize her? No.

Did they ask her out? No.

Did they ask what *she* was wearing, so they could match *her*? No.

Did they ever do anything but telephone? No.

She could not say one more time, "Poor Heath," or "Oh, Heath, I'm so sorry, that's so awful." She could not even manage, "Mmmmmmm."

"Oh, God, Mariss," said Heath from Manhattan, "and my father's putting on weight. He eats when he's nervous. He's not just going to be a crook, he's going to be a *fat* crook."

Marissa began having a tantrum alone in her own room. She drummed her feet violently against the sideboards of her bed. The bed began inching across the room as she attacked it, and she had to scoot along on her back to catch up with it and drum some more. "Heath!" she screamed. "Who *cares*? Noboby cares! Do you hear me? This is boring!"

There was no sound except the sound of her shoes whacking the sideboards. Heath finally mumbled, "I—I wouldn't have bothered you—I thought—well—"

"Talk about something real," shrieked Marissa. "Tell me about class. What you wore. How the team did. Whether you're renting a movie for the ▪▪R tonight. *Stop telling me about your father's trial!*"

Her voice echoed in the phone and around her room. The bed was out of reach. She was off the rug and onto the dust kittens that had moments ago been hidden by the bed. This is one of my best friends on the phone, thought Marissa. What I just said to him was awful.

She tried to think of an apology, and then became enraged all over again. Why should *she* apologize? It was Heath's fault, he was so self-centered. She didn't care how hard his life was; she was much more interested in how hard *her* life was.

In Manhattan, Heath took a deep breath.

In Rye, Marissa slammed the phone down. Clouds of dust kittens danced around the shivering cord.

For quite a while she lay on the floor, wanting to call Heath back and never wanting to call him back. Hoping he would call her and hoping he would never call her. She was still lying there when the phone rang and it was Sin, to say his dad was letting him take the good car, and he could drive Marissa to the Hilton, and was she spending the night at the hotel?

"Yes, I'm staying over. The wedding's at eight, and I doubt if the reception will be over till long after midnight, and I want to stay up all night anyhow talking to Vi." If Vi's coming, thought Marissa. If she wants to talk to me, too.

They discussed gray and cream and dark red and who else would be there and wouldn't it be great to see everybody again. "Heath call you yet tonight?" Sin asked, because he knew his Mondays. Sin li to be kept up to date on Heath's situation.

Marissa had promised Heath she would never

tell any details of his problems. But her crush on Sin was so great that she offered the news so that Sin would keep calling.

I am scum, thought Marissa. The bottom of a stagnant pond. Algae growing on my moral values. Oil slicks on my friendships.

I, Marissa, who prided myself on being the best possible counselor, the girl on whom they could all model themselves—clean, honest, true, dependable, generous, kind, and courteous—I am the one who passes on gossip and abandons a friend in need.

Marissa skipped Sin's question about Heath calling and described the outfit she and her mother had finally found. Sin thought it sounded perfect. "You'll be beautiful, Mariss," he said affectionately. "You and I will look terrific together."

But it was not balm to her soul. Her soul felt too lousy for mere balm. It needed major surgery.

She wished she could talk to Violet about it. But she had neither written to Vi nor phoned her, not once since camp ended. They had hugged good-bye so intensely! Promised to be forever friends, saying this as one word—inextricably entwined: *foreverfriends*.

And they had not communicated once.

Was it that camp was so precious it had to remain enclosed in its summer time-space?

Or had they known in their hearts they were not foreverfriends but only summer friends?

Marissa yearned for Vi, silly frothy Vi, with her hot rollers and her cases of eye makeup and her frilly clothes for any occasion, even though the only occasion had been campfire. And yet she dreaded Vi. Was Vi, away from camp, sort of embarrassing?•Would Vi's chatter, so comical and endearing at camp, be blather elsewhere?

What if they hugged hello—and they were strangers?

Marissa had never been to any kind of reunion. When you first thought of it, it was the warmest image possible. All hugs and laughter, joy and pleasure.

Then loopholes pierced the dream. There might be nothing to talk about. They might have nothing in common but hanging up their regulation blue tank suits to dry, or smushing down their graham crackers to make S'mores.

She thought of calling Vi quickly, before the reunion. But you couldn't just phone a person you had ignored for three months.

What if the other girls had been in touch all along? What if Violet had written to the others, and gone to parties with them, and been on the phone with them? What if Vi's mailbox had been full of letters from buddies at camp, while nobody had even considered writing to Marissa?

And what—worst of all—if she did not matter even to Sin? Perhaps Marissa was Sin's shield. He could not very well wear his trademark wraparound sunglasses at the wedding, so he would wear Marissa. Sin's crush had been on Cathy, who had ignored Sin all summer in favor of Trevor and Brandon. Sin had followed Cathy lik puppy, hoping for anything, even a kick, that would show Cathy'd noticed him. He got the kick on the last day, when Cathy turned out to have a serious boyfriend from home she had never gotten around to mentioning.

Perhaps Sin was afraid to face Cathy, and that was his only reason for wanting to match Marissa and go together.

Marissa decided not to go. She couldn't face Cathy, either. Cathy possessed a beauty so demanding you could not stop staring. It hooked you, with barbs. And then Cathy would humiliate you, and people laughed at you, and you crumbled in public.

I could call Heath back, Marissa thought. But Heath—even if he accepted her apologies—had lost any ability to have fun. Marissa wanted to be with Sin, who considered it his duty in life to have fun.

She had spent her summer engineering other people's fun, and this had been fine, because that was what camp counselors did. But it was not fair to continue it in the fall.

Oh, what will I do? thought Marissa miserably. How am I going to face all these people? I'm not the girl I pretended to be at camp. I'm not good and sweet and perfect. I can't even write my best girlfriend or be kind to my second-best boyfriend.

But then she remembered that Cathy despised them all and laughed at the idea of camp. Cathy would never come.

With that burden gone, Marissa could breathe again and, just a little bit, began to get excited about going to the reunion after all.

5

―――

Claudia's plans took shape.

If she were to be gone for a weekend, and neither parent know, she had to have places to stay at night. Claudia had no interest in park benches in the winter. She got her best friend, Lynn, to invite her to stay at her house on Friday night. That was good because Lynn's house was near the center of town and the railroad station, and Lynn's parents always slept till noon on Saturday. They would never know that instead of being driven home by a parent, Claudia had walked downtown to take a train alone.

Saturday she would be going to the Hilton for the reunion, and since the wedding itself was in the evening, with a reception afterward, it would end very late. It was reasonable, therefore, to spend Saturday night at the Hilton.

Claudia got the phone number of the hotel from

the operator. In her deepest, most mature voice, she called to make a room reservation. Claudia had never been so proud of herself. She requested a single room for the night for Miss Claudia Goodman, and the voice replied, "Certainly, madam."

Claudia loved that. *Madam*. And her parents didn't even know! She hugged it to herself. A secret revenge. All the little games they had played on her—and now she could play a few moves on them. She liked being the only one to know. It gave her quite a feeling of superiority. She—their thirteen-year-old child—would be on her own in another town for two days and a night and they would never even know. They, who prided themselves on being the perfect parents.

She packed her suitcase carefully. For the reunion itself she would wear her favorite torn jeans, her old sneakers, and her beloved Camp Men sweatshirt, faded now from many washings. For the wedding, the bridesmaid dress from her mother's wedding. This was a floor-length lemon yellow satin with many ruffles and bows and a long sash, with an overlay of ivory lace like a Victorian apron. It swished and whispered when she moved.

She added food. It might be a Hilton hotel, but you always needed your own food supply. She had learned that at camp. Claudia put in Mallomars, Cheetos, and Oreos. That should last for a night. She would stay awake all night watching forbidden movies on TV and eating cookies in bed and laughing because Daddy and Heather Anne and Mommy and Jonathan wouldn't even know.

And if they should find out, by some chance, and suddenly realize at dawn that none of them had Claudia, well, that would be rather pleasant, too. Claudia did not mind at all if they panicked and called the FBI and got ready to pay ransoms.

When she arrived at Lynn's house, Lynn's mother burst out laughing. "Why, Claudia Goodman, that's the largest *overnight* bag I've ever seen in my life. How long are you planning to stay with us? Two years?"

Claudia managed to smile politely.

Upstairs Lynn opened the suitcase and began rifling through it. "Oooooh, look! It's your bridesmaid dress! Are we going to play dress-up? Oooooh, neat!"

Claudia liked to think she had left such childish games behind. But she didn't want to explain anything to Lynn, so she said Lynn could put the dress on. After a huge supper of leftover turkey and stuffing, cranberry sauce, and gravy, the girls went back upstairs so Lynn could practice being a bridesmaid. "Whose house were you at for Thanksgiving?" asked Lynn, who found divorce very exciting.

"Both. I stayed at Daddy's on Wednesday. Then we all went to a restaurant on Thursday, and I went back to Mommy's after," said Claudia. She hated admitting she'd eaten Thanksgiving dinner in a restaurant. It was saying out loud, *we are not a family, we are people who eat out on holidays*. But Lynn was filled with envy, and it is always nice to be envied, so Claudia made up lots of details about how terrific the restaurant was.

First thing in the morning Claudia was up and into her jeans and sweatshirt (so large it reached her knees) and packing her suitcase.

"You're not walking?" said Lynn, when Claudia prepared to leave. "Claudia, you live miles from here. Wait till noon and Mom will be up to drive you."

Claudia insisted on leaving.

"Are you mad at me?" said Lynn anxiously.

"No, I have a train to catch."

Now Lynn was really impressed. She put on her coat and helped Claudia pull the suitcase. It had two tiny wheels at one end and a stiff handle at the other. It was like yanking a dog along on a very short leash.

The weather was very cold. Claudia zipped up her ski jacket, festooned with last year's chair lift tickets. She had forgotten mittens and scarf. She shivered.

"Where's the train to?" asked Lynn as they waited on the platform.

Claudia thought. "Boston," she said finally.

"Oh, my goodness! Who are you going to see? Relatives? New ones you got with Heather Anne or Jonathan?"

Claudia was grateful for this suggestion. "Yes. Heather Anne's sister—um—Vivian—is having me for a while. Vivian is—um—a vet, and I can play with all her dogs. And ponies."

"Wow," said Lynn. "And you're going to Boston the train all by yourself?"

"Sure."

Lynn was not allowed to go to the YWCA to

48

swim by herself, let alone Boston by train. Claudia waved good-bye to Lynn, being relaxed and superior, although she had only been on a train twice herself, as whenever the Goodmans had gone to New York or Boston, they'd driven.

When Lynn was out of sight, the adventure began to count. Nobody knows where I am! exulted Claudia, staring out the grimy window. When the train arrived at her station, she got off, signaled a taxi, and arrived quickly at the Hilton. She was a little surprised by how much this transportation cost, but shrugged. She had fifty dollars birthday money, so there was no problem.

A gleaming maroon-and-gold doorman opened the hotel door for her. He looked like an usher at a wedding, only more colorful.

The lobby was fantastic. Claudia abandoned her suitcase for a moment just to peek around and explore. Thick vermilion carpet with gold-key trim led down corridors that stretched away like those in airline terminals. The vast lobby was divided by gleaming marble columns rising two stories, and by flower arrangements as big as pianos.

Claudia darted past a very long, wooden check-in desk, at which dozens of people were crowded, and where phones rang continually and demandingly. Beyond the ranks of elevators and small shops selling imported perfumes and newspapers, the interior of the Hilton suddenly opened up. An enormous room, as big and as high as a school gym, was crisscrossed by silver balconies hanging from silver ropes. Climbing like spider webs into the vaulted, skylit ceiling, the silver stairs seemed hung by tinsel from starry chandeliers.

Claudia was entranced.

She took the steps two at a time. A chandelier hung temptingly close to the junction of stairs and balcony. Had nobody ever swung from it? Claudia was confident she could find a Camp Men alum who would give it a try.

Claudia hopped back down the stairs and located her suitcase. It was still beside an enormous red leather sofa kind of thing—circular—with palms growing in the middle. The sofa would be useful if you had twenty friends who wanted to sit with their backs to each other.

Claudia sat for a while, watching people come and go. She was particularly taken by two, very thin, elegant ladies, each of whom had a very thin, elegant dog on a jeweled leash. Claudia preferred dogs that could knock down letter carriers.

Claudia was quite hungry. She should have had breakfast with Lynn, but she had forgotten food in the rush to be away before Lynn's parents were awake. A large, dark olive green sign said in twisted gold script that there were a total of six restaurants in the hotel, to suit any taste. Claudia wondered which one would suit a taste for Special K and bananas?

First she'd check in. Investigate her room. See if there were any of those free things she loved that her father brought back when he traveled—small ckets of hand lotion or shampoo.

Claudia waited in line at the high, gleaming check-in desk, finally giving her name to the young woman at the computer terminal. The computer printed out Claudia's name on her bill. Claudia was thrilled. She had never had her very own bill before. She loved that: the officialness of being Claudia Goodman, hotel guest.

"And how are you going to pay, Miss Goodman?" said the woman.

"I have cash," Claudia said proudly.

The woman smiled. "Fine. Your room will be number eight-fifty-five, but I am afraid it's not yet vacant. You may get the key at about noon. The price of the room is one hundred seventy dollars, and you must check out before eleven tomorrow morning. We'll check your luggage for you until the room is available." She rang an old-fashioned bell, and a very old man tottered up to take Claudia's suitcase, giving her a pink plastic ticket to reclaim it.

One hundred and seventy dollars? thought Claudia. For one room? For one night?

She did not dare ask if this could be the wrong price. She could not bring herself to admit she did not have even a third of that amount.

The businessman behind Claudia sighed with impatience. The family on her right eyed her Camp Men sweatshirt with interest. The man on her left bumped her leg with his briefcase, apologized without looking at her, and hurried away. The check-in clerk waited calmly.

If she said she couldn't afford the room after all, would the clerk ask questions? Would she ma█ Claudia phone her parents? What *was* she going to do for the night now?

Claudia was desperately afraid she was going to cry. She could just imagine the telephone call home. How they would tell her she was childish and silly, irritating and uncooperative. How they would laugh at her, and punish her. How they would tell their cocktail guests what she had tried to do. ("And can you imagine, Florence, the child actually thought she could stay at the Hilton for fifty dollars?" . . . Gales of laughter.)

Claudia's heart hurt and her chest grew tight. She remembered her excuse to Lynn. "You know what? My aunt Vivian is really going to pay for the room when she gets here. Maybe I won't check in now. When Aunt Vivian gets here, she'll do it for both of us."

The check-in clerk nodded without interest. "What's your Aunt Vivian's last name?"

"Bskxpyvk," said Claudia quickly, and she gripped her luggage ticket and fled. Luckily the lobby was jammed with people going in and out, and her flight was covered by pin-striped suits and mink coats. Claudia disappeared down a hallway. She ducked into a telephone booth to hide, but when she shut the door the light went on, so she left the door open. The inside was upholstered, like a restaurant booth.

I'm not giving up my adventure, thought Claudia. I'm not phoning home for help. I'll figure something out. And I'm not telling anybody now, because they'd find out about that awful thing at the desk. I'll never let anybody know about that.

She decided that, later on, she would use this

phone and pretend to be Aunt Vivian, canceling Claudia Goodman's reservation.

Farther down the same hall was the Country Squire, A Family-Style Café. Claudia checked out the menu. Toast, eggs, grapefruit, orange juice, and coffee were seven dollars. Oh, well, thought Claudia recklessly. She ordered the biggest breakfast on the menu.

It was ten in the morning.

The reunion began at two.

6

All right, said Cathy to herself as she got into the taxi and asked for the railroad station. I will not flirt. I will not demand attention. I will not steal the show. I will not alienate any girls. I will be nice. I will be patient and generous—

Who, me? she thought. That's like trying to take off fifty pounds in one day.

All right. I'll make two rules and stick to them. One. No flirting. Two. No grandstand shows to get attention. Or even little minor shows to get attention.

Great, thought Cathy, fishing in her purse for the taxi fare. If I don't get their attention, nobody'll speak to me. What good is it going to a reunion if nobody speaks to me?

She smoothed her dress. A plain, dark crimson wool sheath, no jewelry except small, gold hoop earrings. Touch of makeup. Flat dull shoes. Cathy had always been able to analyze her looks correctly, and she knew that, although it had been her intention to dress down, she was even more beautiful with less.

Perhaps you could climb out of bad habits. You could not climb out of your own body.

Cathy had hope—not much, but a little—for the reunion. When she'd telephoned the hotel to make her reservation, the clerk had told her that a Camp Menunkechogue party of three had booked a suite for four and needed someone to fill the fourth slot. Would she like to have it? Yes, she said quickly, hoping her roommate would be the girls with whom she could start her new personality.

But what if they knew her? Suppose one of them was Marissa? Or Vi? Those two would cancel their reservations if they found they had to share a room with Cathy Coatsworth. She'd be alone in a four-person suite.

Cathy climbed on the train and sat alone. She was alone in her heart and alone in her thoughts. The blue sky and brisk autumn wind meant nothing to her. She felt nothing, knew nothing. Except loneliness.

By noon, Claudia had checked out the British Hunt Room (oil paintings of dogs chasing foxes, thick furniture, and food that looked equally heavy). She had walked up all ten flights of stairs in the hotel, and ridden in every elevator. She had investigated the three little shops (boring) and wandered into the IBM meeting room to see if she could blend in. She could not.

She was sauntering through the front lobby for the umpteenth time when she realized that somebody was eyeing her very suspiciously. Not a uniformed bellboy or doorman, but a thin, frowning man in a fine dark suit, with a flower in his lapel. Claudia thought she had better avoid him, but he blocked her way.

"Hi, there," said Claudia sweetly. Attack is always better than defense, she reasoned. "Do you by any chance know where the Camp Menunkechogue reunion is to be held, and could you show me the way?"

"Oh, you're here for the camp reunion." The man laughed. "Of course, I should have guessed. It's not actually scheduled till two, of course, but I believe the man in charge is setting up. Follow the silver stairs, cross the hanging balcony, and the Mayflower Room is third on your right."

Claudia bounded away, as if joining a volleyball team at camp. The man in charge, sure enough, was Charles, mixing paint.

"Charles," said Claudia severely, "this is your wedding day. Can't you think of anything better to do?"

Charles laughed. "Hello, Claudia. You're my first alum. Good to see you. Here, help the waiter with that tablecloth."

So Claudia helped with hanging vast, white linen cloths on huge tables, and unfolding chairs, and centering flowers, and rolling in moving coat racks. There is nothing like being useful to take your mind off your troubles, and Claudia momentarily forgot that she had a big problem coming that night.

She took a message from one of the hotel staff to the linen rooms, and coming back she was gratified to find four Camp Men boys on the balcony, pummeling each other, screaming, and threatening to toss each other over the side. They dared her to catch them. Claudia tossed her hair and turned away. The boys yodeled after her, and then suddenly shouted the great, all-time warning, "Counselor coming! Counselor coming!"

Vi! thought Claudia. It's got to be Vi!

Laughing, overjoyed, already running, she searched for the counselor. There, below her on the silver stairs, was the unmistakable golden head of the one counselor Claudia had truly despised.

Cathy Coatsworth.

Sin had been allowed to take his father's Jaguar, and he was so proud of himself in that terrific sports car, he could hardly see straight. He definitely could not see Marissa. He did not even notice how carefully she had picked out clothing to match his—gray and dark red and cream. Her crimson sweater perfectly set off her thick dark hair, and the deep gray skirt and cream-and-black scarf, made her feel more sophisticated than she had ever felt in her life. She did not feel like a teenager going to a camp reunion but like an adult going to her first job.

"Hi, Mriss!" said Sin. "Get this car! Fantastic, huh? Dad bought it this summer, and as long as I keep it in the hotel garage overnight, I get to use it.

I'm almost sorry we have to go to this dumb reunion. Would you rather head north and drive up to Canada? We could see how this baby does under all sorts of traffic conditions!" Sin didn't wait for her answer; he was already in the driver's seat, panting for joy.

I love this jerk? thought Marissa. Who hasn't even spotted me yet? Who wants me in the car only to appreciate his driving skills?

At least she wasn't a cover against Cathy. He might not even see Cathy against the glitter of his Jag. Though Cathy could probably outshine a whole dealership full of Jaguars if she made the effort. And Cathy would always, always, make the effort.

Marissa said, "We look perfect for the wedding, but do you think we're dressed properly for the camp reunion?"

"Aw, Marissa. We're not going to play games and do activities. It won't be camp. We'll circulate, go to the bar and the buffet, show off a little, and find out what everybody's been doing. Wonder what Heath will drive up in? Probably two or three Jaguars at once, with all that money to throw around."

"Sin! You know he hates that money. It's stolen."

"That's what he says to you, anyhow. What else is he going to say, when you think about it? He can hardly tell you he couldn't care less where it came from. He wants you on his side, and you're very moral, Marissa."

Oh, yeah, she thought. I, who tell you Heath's secrets and can't be bothered to listen to his problems, I'm very moral.

But nobody would know she wasn't. She and Sin would circulate and converse, and everybody would think that Marissa in her crimson and gray was the wholesome embodiment of Camp Menunkechogue girls.

"If he's not driving up in a Jag, how *is* Heath getting here?" said Sin.

Marissa admitted she didn't know.

"I thought you talked to him all the time. Is he even coming at all?"

Marissa didn't know that, either.

"I guess I misjudged this," said Sin, and he actually looked at her for a moment. It's only because we're ten cars back from a red light, Marissa thought cynically. "I thought you and Heath were as close as the bark on a tree," added Sin.

Heath had thought so, too. Expected her to nurse his wounds, put Band-Aids on his cuts. Never asked for her living, breathing, visible company, though. So who was close to whom? Or was that one of the things you never knew in life?

Marissa shrugged and looked out the window. They were in a cement cavern approaching the turnpike entrance. She read the graffiti and regretted it.

"Say. Is this the Camp Men girl we all knew and loved?" teased Sin. "Sulking out the window?"

"You never knew me at all, Sinclair Franklin!" said Marissa sharply. "Or loved me, either. You didn't even notice—" She bit off her sentence. To finish it would be begging for compliments.

Sin had stopped looking at her, anyway. The

light had turned green; he was out of the traffic, surging up the entrance ramp to the turnpike, passing a station wagon, leaping between a moving van and a Datsun, getting into the third lane, and passing the speed limit, all in about sixty seconds. "What a car!" Sin murmured contentedly to himself.

Marissa sat forgotten on his right. She tried mentally to take her crush on Sin, throw it out the window, and have it be run over by all the million cars on the turnpike.

Heather Anne said to her husband, "Oh, darling, look. Claudia left her schoolbooks here at Thanksgiving. I know she has that report to write and she'll need this whole stack. Why don't you run them over to the other house."

They both hated going to the other house.

Claudia's father said, "Why don't *you* run them over, darling? I've really got so much to do."

"But my friends are due any moment, darling. I really have to be here."

Claudia's father frowned. "I'm not sure we should bail her out so frequently. She has to learn to keep track of her own possessions, and perhaps a bad grade would teach her a lesson." The thought of Claudia having a bad grade actually upset him very much. But not enough to take the books straight over to the other house.

After Heather Anne's guests arrived, and conversation slowed down, and the dear old friends ran out of things to say, he knew it was just a matter of minutes before he would take the books over after all.

It's the kind of hotel that's meant to intimidate, Vi thought, approaching the building.

Immensely high ceilings sparkled with distant chandeliers. Uniformed doormen regarded each person who approached with great contempt or with great respect.

The doorman, Violet told herself, is a stranger. I do not care in the slightest whether he treats me with respect or contempt.

This was a lie. She desperately wanted the doorman to be impressed. To treat her better than he would the common run of guests.

She was wearing the clothes of Jasmine's choice, clothes not quite right for her own petite figure. Soft black leather boots ended high under a long clingy skirt of fine black wool. Jasmine's four gold-rope necklaces rested on a long, belted Viyella shirt of a blurry dark gold, brown, and red. A thick wool scarf picked up the red and lay casually on her shoulders to set off her yellow curls. In her heart, Vi knew you needed to be five foot nine to wear the outfit. Vi was five one.

She was carrying her ski jacket because, although it was frigid out, the ski jacket was pink and looked ridiculous with the sophisticated clothes. She tried to crunch up the jacket so nobody could spot it, but the thick down stuffing spread through her fingers and oozed out like rising bread dough. The doorman smiled broadly as he held open the lobby door.

Vi stalked behind a flower arrangement so large it could have been divided among several hospitals. In the shade of gladiolus taller than she was, Vi struggled to stow the ski jacket out of sight. Hordes of beautiful people strolled by, leisurely in their wealth and style. Other beautiful people dashed about at great speed, giving off an aura of power and urgency.

Vi just knew Jamie was going to appear when she had her purse handle in her mouth and was trying to cram the ski jacket down into her makeup case.

Farther on, between Vi and the enormous reception desks, was a meeting board. Large and black, it used small white letters on black ledges to announce locations.

AMA, 3rd floor West, Shore Room
Welcome IBM! Main Lounge check-in
SUNY, info, Room 612

Nothing about Camp Menunkechogue.

Great, thought Vi. I have the wrong day.

Next to her, a group of attractive men and women, executive types carrying briefcases and wearing company name tags, burst into laughter. "How do you pronounce *that*?"

"I haven't seen a T-shirt like that since I was nine years old!"

How could she have missed it! Not content with mere black and white, Charles had brought a six-foot tall, green sandwich board. Pinned to the sides were boys' and girls' T-shirts with the camp logo on them, and in shrieking red Magic Marker, the huge words.

CAMP MENUNKECHOGUE REUNION!!!!!!
HI, GUYS!!!
WELCOME ABOARD. WEAR YOUR T-SHIRTS.
COME ONE****COME ALL!!!
MAYFLOWER ROOM 2ND FLOOR
LOTS OF GOOD GAMES AND ACTIVITIES PLANNED!!!!!

Nobody will come, thought Vi. Only little kids. Eight-year-olds. I didn't hear from anybody because nobody else would lower themselves. If they're going to the wedding, they'll show up at eight tonight, not for Charles's games and fun activities.

I was the only one stupid enough to come.

7

————

Alicia was alone in her room at the Hilton for the first time in days. Her mother, her friends, Charles of course, her bridesmaids, everybody involved with the details of a large wedding had hovered around, accomplishing things or getting in the way. But now she was alone.

Alicia opened the closet door at the far end of her room. It was a lovely room: the walls a sort of damask, the bedspreads something that gleamed, the mirrors bright and trimmed in gold. But she cared nothing for it. It was the closet that counted.

She took out her wedding gown. Very carefully she laid it on the bed, and then she sat next to it, and touched its soft silken fabric, and ran her fingers over the lace, and circled the hundreds of tiny, tiny pearls.

My wedding gown. My perfect day.

Charles. My husband.

She had had to take off her eye makeup because she was so happy she kept crying. This had never happened to Alicia before: tears of joy. Her eyes were puffy. She didn't even care. They would clear up by eight tonight when she appeared before her wedding guests . . . and Charles, dear Charles, stood at the far end of the aisle.

Her favorite color was pale peach and she had chosen it for her four bridesmaids, with a deeper, rosier peach for her maid of honor, and flowers in cascades—roses in the deeper color, with ferns and baby's breath and stephanotis and ribbons that would curl and hang low and dance around the girls' long dresses as they walked so slowly toward Charles.

The wedding consultant had said that peach as a color was a bit out of season, and Alicia had said it was *her* season and she would have peach if she wanted peach and that was that.

I'm getting married, thought Alicia.

It was such a lovely and perfect thought that there was room for nothing else in her mind. When her travel alarm went off, she couldn't believe it. Now she was going to have to appear at the camp reunion.

Well, Mother was right, thought Alicia. It was dumb to combine the camp reunion with the wedding. I cannot think about two things like that at one time. I will have to go downstairs to the Mayflower Room and talk with old campers about rashes and sunburns we have known, about twisted ankles I have treated, and campfire songs we have sung together.

The only togetherness I want is with Charles.

Four hours of camp reunion. Yes, Mother, you're right, we're crazy.

But, Alicia reflected, she would be crazy like this many more times in her life. Charles owned the two Menunkechogue camps: boys and girls all the way around the lovely little gem of a Maine lake. Every summer till they were old and gray (and maybe then, too), she and Charles would return to Maine to run Camp Menunkechogue for Boys and Camp Menunkechogue for Girls.

Alicia pulled on her jeans. She added a Camp Men sweatshirt. How ridiculous to be purposely putting this on only hours before her own wedding. She would have to leave the reunion early to have her hair done, and then come back to her room to slide into her wedding gown.

While she was laughing, sitting on the bed stroking her gown, Charles knocked and entered. He was wearing red shorts and a Camp Men T-shirt. He looked rather silly, as he always did when dressed like one of his campers, and yet just right, as if born to the T-shirt the way princes are born to the purple. Alicia jumped up to kiss and hug him. "I love you, Charles."

He was uncomfortable with bold declarations like that. He said, "We've got to go on down to the Mayflower Room. The kids are starting to arrive."

"You go down. I'll join you later."

"But you're all ready. Come on."

"I have to put away my gown."

"I'll wait while you hang it up."

"It takes longer than that," explained Alicia. "I have to enjoy putting it away."

Charles sighed and said okay he understood, although obviously he didn't, and he set off for the Mayflower Room. Alicia touched the gown twice more before her cousins, who were to be brides-maids, burst in on her with their hugs and kisses and congratulations and giggles.

Marissa was astonished to run into Trevor and Brandon. They had been counselors with Sin, but she had had little contact with them, and they had vanished from her memory. And yet here they were, like Sin, in street clothes. She recalled them in bathing trunks and untied sneakers, knew their muscles and legs and tans, knew that Brandon wore a gold chain and Trevor had a long white scar from an old abdominal surgery. Today each wore cords, a good shirt, a fine pullover sweater—and wonder of wonders—polished leather shoes. "Wow," said Marissa in greeting. "Real shoes? With a shine? I'm all excited."

She was not excited in the least, merely sur-prised that Trevor and Brandon were alive, that their lives had continued to go on, when she had excused them from existence.

"Marissa!" shouted Trevor, hugging her. "Great to see you again! You look wonderful!"

Brandon kissed her as well as hugged her. "How've you been?" he demanded, as if he had been nervous since August, wondering whether she was okay.

Kissing the strangers. Awkward with the loved one.

Was this perhaps what a reunion consisted of?

Facile affection with people you hardly remembered, and dread over meeting your friends?

Trevor and Brandon shook hands with Sin, and the boys walloped each other on the back, and laughed, and ran out of things to say.

Marissa wondered if Cathy had gone out with Trevor or Brandon ever again. Cathy had had them on each side of her, the way you might have horses for an old-fashioned carriage: the dark one offset by the light one, matched in weight and stride.

"So who else is coming?" said Sin, as if sixty seconds had used up his attention span for Trevor and Brandon, and now he was ready for the interesting people.

"Cathy is," said Trevor. "I checked the RSVP list on the Mayflower Room wall. Wait'll you see that meeting room. Charles has got photographs of the camp in winter, and they're creepy. It's not like anything you remember."

Marissa's heart sank, and not over the condition of Camp Men in winter. What would gray and cream and crimson be against the silver and gold cruelty of Cathy Coatsworth?

"Heath coming?" Brandon asked her.

He'll be Heath forever, now, Marissa thought. His Camp nickname—Dark—is gone. It made him soft and remote, to be called Dark. But he's Heath now, and his real personality is harsh and desperate. "I don't know," she told Brandon.

"God, I hope so," said Brandon. "I've really been following that case. I even started reading the *Wall Street Journal* every day because it's got the most detailed coverage."

"But not the goriest," said Trevor, listing the papers he liked to read to get the really juicy details on the family.

"They had to sell their Lake Placid summer place to pay lawyers' fees."

"Get out of town. They have millions stashed away. They don't have to sell a single silver spoon."

"Sure they do. That way they can pretend to be broke and pitiful, but when the whole thing cools off, they'll go to Luxembourg or something and live on what they've got in banks in Europe."

Was this what Heath had to listen to each day? Marissa wondered. An analysis of the family tricks?

"I'll tell you guys a few details that will make your hair stand on end," said Sin.

"No!" cried Marissa. "Sin—you—you can't!"

Brandon and Trevor said if Sin had a scoop he should sell it. Somebody besides Heath Hesper senior should make a buck out of this; newspapers were willing to pay for those details and Sin could make a classical buck.

Marissa took Sin's hand and held it tightly, as if she could press out of his skin any desire to make money off her gossip. "Sin, let's go up to Reception. I have to get my room key. And I have to set my bag down somewhere." She hauled him off with her. "Sin," she whispered, "you just can't tell them the things I told you. They're secrets."

"No, they're not. You told me."

"But—but, Sin, Heath trusted me not to."

He stared at her. Then he grinned. "Okay. I'll just tell the papers, not Brandon and Trevor."

Marissa almost cried out. She looked back at the two boys, but she had no sense of their personalities. They seemed too much alike to be human. Even their names were smooth and hard to get hold of. What might they do to Heath?

"I was kidding," said Sin. "Heath is my friend, too, Marissa."

"It's that—oh, Sin, you said Heath wants to be moral around me because I'm moral—but Sin, I'm not. I gossip."

"Aw, Marissa, don't take it to heart so much." He put his arm around her, and pressed her head against one of his broad shoulders, and she felt ridiculous rather than comforted. "I just wanted to be in step with Trev and Brandon," said Sin. "All this reunion feeling overcame my better half, see. But now I'm with you, I'll be good. You have that effect on people. We all behave with you."

Marissa was sick of boys behaving with her. She glared at the reception-desk clerk who jumped, wondering what was wrong.

"You go on up and get rid of your suitcase," said Sin. "I'll meet you in the Mayflower Room."

"Sin, you promise you won't talk about Heath?"

"Promise." He kissed her on the lips, a long, sealing-wax sort of kiss. The people waiting to check in smiled indulgently, and Trevor and Brandon yodeled in appreciation, and Marissa blushed hotly.

She was filled to the brim with intense desires. That Sin should fall in love with her, that Vi should

71

still be a friend, that Heath should forgive her, that the reunion should be a smashing success. She felt as if she were toeing the starting line of a major race, without knowing the track or the prize.

Don't take it to heart so much, Sin had said.

A fundamental difference between boys and girls. Marissa always took things to heart.

Let a boy take me to his heart, she thought. Tonight.

Lynn and her mother had a typical and completely boring Saturday. A morning of cartoons for Lynn, until her parents finally got up, and then Lynn had lunch while they had breakfast.

Lynn and her mother started the laundry (Lynn's mother worked, and had to do all the housework on Saturday, or not at all), and the washing machine wouldn't go. Lynn's father was busy fixing the storm windows that he hadn't gotten to when the weather first got cold and could not attack the washing machine. Lynn and her mother loaded the laundry into the car, drove away, remembered detergent and bleach, drove back, went to the laundromat, and had to wait an hour for machines to be free.

Lynn guarded their place in line while her mother did errands: pharmacy, photography shop, dry cleaner's and the Salvation Army store to drop off old boots. Lynn's mother got back just as Lynn finished stuffing sheets into a machine at one end of the laundromat, cold-water whites into another machine at the opposite end, and hot-water whites into a machine in the middle, and was waiting for some creature in polyester pants to finish getting her stuff out of another machine, so Lynn could do the jeans and darks in it.

Lynn hated laundry. She hated laundromats and all people who used them. She hated Saturdays.

She and her mother sat on orange plastic seats to watch their laundry swirl behind glass doors. "I hate laundry," said Lynn's mother. "I hate laundromats. I hate Saturdays."

They giggled. Lynn kept thinking of Claudia's Saturday.

"It's so neat being divorced," said Lynn. "You get all these new relatives. Now, Claudia has this terrific aunt, Wendy, or Gertrude, or something, who keeps ponies in Boston."

"I would rather have an Aunt Gertrude who did the laundry for me," said her mother.

Lynn said her family was really quite dull and she never got to have any new relatives. Her mother said maybe Lynn would get lucky, and marry into a family full of people who kept ponies in Boston.

The clothes finished washing. They jammed the wet things into baskets and hauled them back to the car. "Our dryer had better work," said Lynn darkly. "I sure don't want to come back here today."

She looked at her mother for reassurance.

"Do you know that Claudia doesn't do a single household chore?" said Lynn. "Not at her father's house and not at her mother's."

Lynn's mother said nothing.

"And how come I don't get to go alone to big

cities? If you can trust me to do the laundry," Lynn said, "how come you can't trust me to go up to Boston when I feel like it?"

"That is the most ridiculous thing I ever heard. You're twelve. You can't go hundreds of miles to some—I mean—there's crime—or you could get lost—or—I don't know, terrible things could happen."

Lynn made a face. Just once in her life, she would like something terrible to happen. They reached home, each lugging a heavy basket of wet clothes inside.

"You don't mean Claudia went alone to Boston, do you?" said Lynn's mother. "How could she? Didn't her aunt Gertrude or her mother or somebody drive her?"

"Course not. She took the train. By herself. She had her suitcase ready, and we walked to the train station, and she got on the train for Boston."

Lynn's mother stared at her. The stare made Lynn uneasy. She squirmed. "Well, she did, Mother!"

"But, Lynn—the train to Boston doesn't stop here. We're a local station."

8

———

Claudia was at the top of the silver stairs!

Violet forgot Jamie and Marissa and her pink ski jacket and began laughing. She wanted to cry out in celebration! Claudia had come!

Vi was flooded by memories.

Camp—O Camp!

How many nights she and Claudia had sat up together, while the other girls slept. They would eat Twinkies that Vi's mother mailed in and tell each other sad stories. Vi's sad stories were all made-up and Claudia's were all true. Outside, the forest would rasp and creak, the loons on the lake would utter death calls, and Big Foot would trample dry branches. But inside, they were cozy: Claudia sitting up in her sleeping bag like a large navy-blue worm, and Vi wrapped in her blankets like a pink designer caterpillar.

Vi darted up the silver steps, remembering the

cliff walk and how they used to slide down it on their fannies, so you could tell a Violet girl by the condition of her jeans. How Claudia had grown in three short months! From a girl as thin as a bookmark to the first curves of a teenager. Vi couldn't wait to—

And Cathy strolled across the silver balcony.

Violet would have known Cathy anywhere. That gold hair, too gold to be real, cascading over the slim shoulders, gleaming like precious metal against the well-chosen, simple, dark wool of Cathy's sophisticated dress. Cathy stood in the midst of the glittering chandeliers and outshone everything there.

Vi's foot stayed where it was.

Her boots seemed too large, her dress too old for her, her colors wrong. Vi would have to walk up toward Cathy, as if toward a golden goddess, and when she arrived, Cathy would be tall and beautiful and Vi would be short and dowdy.

There was nothing worse than being the right person inside the wrong clothes. You could not show off your personality when your clothes got in the way. Vi didn't care what anybody said; in the wrong clothes, you were the wrong person.

Vi swallowed, took another step, and steeled herself. Cathy, with her splendidly vicious timing, would want details on Jamie. This is it, thought Vi. The most hateful, petty, mean person at Camp Men, will now set me up as her victim-of-the-reunion.

And then Claudia—*her* Claudia—kissed Cathy hello.

How great was the power of a hug!

For the entire two seconds of its duration, Cathy was once more whole, the self-hatred erased.

"Why, Claudia," she said, almost weeping with gladness, "how are you? I'm so glad to see you."

But Claudia pulled herself away as if Cathy had been a telephone pole to chain a bike to, and said, "There's Roxanne. And Dana!" Claudia bolted across the balcony to attack a couple of girls who did not look even vaguely familiar to Cathy.

She was afraid to follow Claudia. The girls were in a huddle, like a human tepee. Cathy felt excluded just watching it. If she went over there and they ignored her, she would lose even the two seconds' joy that the unexpected hug had provided. She could not imagine what had made Claudia hug her, but the aftershock still comforted her, and she clung to it as a child to a teddy bear.

Two seconds is a start, Cathy told herself. If I double it each time, next I'll feel good for four seconds. Heck, before you know it, I'll have experienced a quarter of a minute of happiness.

She turned away, trying to retain the warmth of a hug against the sterile glitter of the huge room, and looked down at the only color—the vermilion carpet two stories below.

There stood Channing's best friend.

Channing had always called him Pink, because his cheeks were oddly red, as if he had poorly applied a lot of rouge. He was very slim, almost weedy, but wore wonderful clothes, and blew his hair dry so that it haloed around his head and fell lightly over the tops of his horn-rimmed glasses. Pink always looked studious and rich, as if he went to Yale, or was the younger brother of an English lord.

The police had asked her if she knew any of Channing's partners, but she'd said no, of course not, and Channing had agreed that of course Cathy didn't know anybody.

For all his chatter to the police, Channing had, in the end, given remarkably little information. He'd claimed to be both mastermind and errand boy, all territory his, all work his. The police were skeptical; it had been too big an operation for one person.

I know Pink, thought Cathy now.

Channing wasn't protecting me from the police, she thought. He was protecting Pink.

She did not know Pink's real name, nor his address, nor where he went to school. Why had she never wondered about it? It was just more proof of her boundless conceit.

Pink turned a bit, and peered past a woman in an evening gown, searching for somebody or something. Then he walked a few paces to the left, took a pipe out of his pocket, and began tamping away at it. Cathy was quite sure that Pink did not smoke a pipe. It was a display to kill time.

Or a signal.

Suddenly she thought—*next he'll look up.* He'll see me. No, no, no, no! I came here for a fresh start, not to renew an old ugly criminal acquaintance!

Cathy stumbled along the balcony, trying to stay invisibly in the middle of it. The fire stairs were closer than the elevators, and she scurried up them, feeling rodentlike in her crouched rush.

The hotel stairs were spooky. They had been vacuumed, and dusted, but Cathy felt as if she were the only person to have used them in years. She was suddenly in a vacant building, in another time zone. The carpet muffled her footsteps and the stairwell rose up and up, like in a nightmare. Red was the color of the wallpaper and carpet, and Cathy blended into it, and she ceased to be a person and was just part of the hotel.

She ran out of breath, her leg muscles trembled, and the door to the fifth floor, when she reached it, was very heavy. Fire regulations? she wondered dimly, pushing her entire weight against the door.

It opened two inches silently, unwillingly, as if only *some* people were allowed on the fifth floor and not necessarily Cathy.

A tiny figure in sweatpants, so far down the long long hall she seemed telescoped, was running toward her crying, "Marissa! Marissa!"

She started to say, "No, it's Cathy," when she saw Marissa, standing with her back to Cathy about four rooms away. Even from behind, there was no mistaking Marissa. That thick mane of dark hair, so unexpectedly romantic and soft on Marissa's strong lean body. Marissa always presented a contradiction of soft and strong, so that people wanted to get to know her better and find out which she really was.

"I'm so excited!" Marissa shouted to Alicia, running to meet her. "Are you excited? Are you

ready? Is everything falling into place just perfectly?"

I'm crazy or they are, thought Cathy.

She had forgotten Marissa's excesses of enthusiasm. Even the way Alicia and Marissa hugged
seemed too much for the occasion, as if they had
something else in mind altogether, while Cathy
was just attending a camp reunion. The two girls
half talked and half just made sounds. Crooning,
purring, happy sounds. Reunion murmurs?
thought Cathy. There was something so touch-
ing—so animal about it. They were exploring each
other with touch and look.

Perhaps a reunion was a very basic human need,
like meals or clean hands. To see another person
once more, whom you once loved, required certain
cries and postures.

"Gosh! What great clothes!" said Alicia admir-
ingly. Cathy quite agreed. Marissa was perfectly
dressed—sophisticated colors and cut, but with
her hair left loose and deeply waved.

"Charles made me wear my Camp Men stuff,"
said Alicia, "but you stay in that, Marissa. Don't
even think about getting into a Camp Men T-shirt.
Somebody has to look decent at this reunion. Now
I have to fly. I just want to warn you about one of
your roommates."

Cathy sucked in her breath. No, no, no, no!
Don't warn her against me! Give me a chance!
Please.

"My cousin Brie," said Alicia. "You know how
families are. She's one of the party, I couldn't help

it. You be nice to her the way you always are, okay? Great. 'Bye now."

Cathy sagged so heavily with relief her weight pushed the door open the rest of the way and they turned and saw her. Cathy felt as if her whole life were at stake. "Hi, Marissa. Hi, Alicia."

Marissa stared at her. Woodenly she said, "Hello, Cathy. How have you been?"

"Fine, thank you. I guess—we'll be sharing a room, then."

"You're the one the hotel gave the fourth bed to," said Alicia in an accusing voice.

Cathy wet her lips. If they made noises now, she thought, it would be growls. Maybe a hiss or two.

"Well, as I say, I have to fly. I'll see you both in the Mayflower Room." Alicia walked in the opposite direction, toward the elevators.

Cathy's hands were shaking. For something to do, she attempted to open the door of their room, but she could not get the key in the lock. The key was actually a plastic computer card, and she could not seem to locate the slot it went into. The seconds ticked by. The door remained shut. Cathy felt as if she would stay hunched over the stubborn door while Marissa looked silently on for years.

"I'll do it," said Marissa. Swiftly and efficiently she let them into the room, turned on the lights, and went to the window to check out the view.

It was an enormous room. Huge windows looked out over treetops bare and black against the gray sky, like fork prongs in the clouds. Long brocade curtains in deep forest green framed the window, and the carpet and bedspreads were the same color, with gold fleur-de-lis patterns, giving the room a heavy, queenly French feel, dragging at your heels for a procession. On one side, a double bed was flanked by French provincial white-and-gold chests of drawers. Opposite the double bed were two single beds, separated by similar chests. On each bed rested a small wicker basket of hotel gifts—a taste of chocolates, a drop of perfume.

How like camp it was!

Each girl looked quickly at the beds to analyze the assets and drawbacks of each position—to stake out the best bed before another camper arrived to seize it.

Marissa picked the more isolated single bed, putting her suitcase possessively on top of it.

Cathy was nearly sick with making her decision. It seemed worse than a summit meeting of the Western powers—having to decide between the other single (thus partnering herself with Marissa, who surely had other plans) or taking half the double (thus sharing not just the room but also the bed with somebody who might also be hostile to her).

Perhaps it would be Brie. Cathy set her overnight bag on the double bed, on the bathroom side, as far from Marissa as she could get and glanced up from under her eyelashes to see if this pleased Marissa.

Marissa was still looking out the window.

"How was your autumn?" Cathy said desperately. "Have you seen much of Sin or Heath?"

"A little."

Cathy hunted for another sentence. "I guess I'll fix my hair before I go down," she said.

"Fine," said Marissa. "I'll run on down now."

And Cathy was left alone in the huge room, holding her hairbrush for hair that was perfect already.

9

Vi felt as lonely as a tiny child who cannot see her mother in the Christmas-shopping crowd. Carols may play and Santa may laugh—but nobody holds your hand.

Quietly she turned on the staircase, squeezed between two other guests, and walked away. Get a grip on yourself, she thought. It was only a hug, and after all, that is the definition of a reunion, isn't it? Hugs all around?

But with Cathy? And not only had Claudia vanished as soon as she'd hugged Cathy, but Cathy had stared long and hard past Vi into the crowds below, as if acknowledging Vi's presence was too silly for Cathy to bother with.

Vi took a different route to the Mayflower Room. She had a backache. Vi was always reading about people whose hearts ached, but emotion took Vi between the shoulder blades, like a mugger's knife. I wish I could have a back rub, she thought. Maybe I'll skip the reunion. Go to the hotel masseuse instead.

Jamie had given her a back rub once. She had curled like a cat beneath his strong fingers.

The lump in Vi's throat hardened into an impenetrable cancerous mass. She wouldn't be able to say hello to anybody at the reunion because she would have choked to death.

The Mayflower Room was a hundred times larger than the Mayflower herself had been. Murals of Pilgrims and Cape Cod, cranberry bogs, and Indians planting corn sprawled around the room. The huge chandeliers here, in an attempt to look Puritan, had tiny black shades instead of sparkling prisms of crystal.

The windows faced the water. In late November, few boats were in Long Island Sound. The sea was gray and gloomy, and the wind shredded it into sharp waves and slapped them against the rocks where, in summer, yachts docked.

The room was far too large for the number of people there. It was not cozy. Vi was among the first arrivals, and the few returning campers so far were lost in the vastness of the place. Too bad we really aren't on a tiny ship, thought Vi. Then we'd have to talk to each other; we'd be crammed in rib to rib.

She surveyed the crowd, hoping for a good selection of handsome teenage boys.

So far, there were two knots of kids about nine or ten looking sorry they had come. A few old men who had probably been counselors when Charles's father owned the camp were alone in the middle of the room, pretending to laugh, and three women in their thirties blocked a window.

Smart people knew better than to arrive on time. Nobody with intelligence would show up first. You wanted to slip into a crowd, not stand all alone like an unwanted cheerleader at a nonexistent game.

Vi could not think of where to stand. She could turn her back on the room, stand by the enormous fire in the stone fireplace, pretending to be chilled. She could also pretend to be hungry and wander past the refreshments. Or, of course, she could make friends with a few women twice her age.

Charles yelled, "Vi! Come on over here and meet Mr. Delamere. He was a camper fifty-three years ago, can you believe that?"

Easily, thought Vi, surveying the wrinkles on Mr. Delamere. I'm only surprised it wasn't a hundred years ago. Somehow he was confusing. She had expected recent campers here; people with vivid memories. How could somebody even remember that camp existed when they'd experienced it all that long ago? Or care?

Mr. Delamere began telling her how camp had been in his day. "All boys back then," he informed her. "Girls and suchlike came later."

Vi felt even gloomier. Had nothing changed in fifty-three years? Would girls and suchlike always come later?

"Name tags!" trumpeted Charles. Vi was embarrassed for him, in his red shorts, showing hairy legs that had lost their tan. Charles wrote out her tag for her, in huge letters, a piece of tape that stretched across her entire chest. V I O L E T!! He wrote as if she were shouting out her own name.

Vi turned her back on him to peel the name tag off as quickly as possible.

"Vi, Vi, Vi, Vi, Vi!" screamed Alicia.

Oh, the sound of one's own name in a lonely room!

Vi swung about, hurled herself on Alicia, and they talked at the same time.

"I'm so glad a real person showed up."

"I didn't know what on earth I was going to say all afternoon," agreed Alicia.

"I love your gown, it's so romantic. Did you go into New York for it?" teased Vi.

Alicia stroked her jeans and sweatshirt. "Specially designed for me," she admitted cheerfully. "Actually, Charles would probably love it if I wore this to the wedding. Would you believe he wanted the wedding in Maine? In November? At the camp? By the dock?"

They shuddered simultaneously. Vi tried to imagine the limousines and flowers, minister and bridesmaids, musicians and guests on that rutted road in the icy November winds, the trees stripped bare of leaves, the mountain gaunt. The little cabins shuttered tight and their doors boarded up. All the nets gone from the playing fields, and the boats locked in their shed. With, no doubt, the tenth snow of the season beginning just as the bride arrived.

The vision was so sad that Vi hurt for Charles. Weddings—which were life and love, gaiety and joy forevermore—in a place where joy was planned as a two-week session?

A two week session of love. It was a horrifying thought. Her mother would like it; it would fit right into her theory that there was no reason for weddings as they simply led to divorce, anyway.

"Vi, darling, cheer up. We're going to have a great time this afternoon. Now where is Jamie? I expected to see you coming in on his muscular arm. I want to hear all the details. Who wins the bets? Claudia or Janey? I believe they told you to keep score of the major dates, minor dates, and important kisses."

Vi had to laugh. It all seemed so silly. "Don't ask, Alicia, because Jamie never called me. Not once. It was definitely a summer romance."

Alicia was shocked. "I really thought it was more than that, Vi! Jamie was so attentive! He seemed to adore you. He even let that wasp sting him he was staring after you so hard during field day."

Vi shrugged. She was afraid of crying.

But Alicia could not get off the topic. She was rallying already, making plans for how to bring them back together through a reunion game. She seemed to think this would be very romantic, especially since it was also her wedding day. "Think about your own romance," Vi advised her.

"No, no," said Alicia. "Jamie RSVP'd. He's coming. So we must capitalize on this situation."

Vi hated it when people made you sound like the stock market. She was rescued by, of all people, Trevor, Brandon, and Sin. Trevor hugged her. Brandon bent down to kiss her. Sin picked her up by the waist and held her at eye level before kissing her. It was pretty wonderful, to be fluffy and blond and five foot one and at your camp reunion.

"So how are you?" she said to Trevor.

He said he was fine.

Brandon admitted to being fine also.

Even Sin said he was fine.

"And how are you?" they asked.

Violet was fine.

Nobody had anything else to say. They stood looking away from each other, as if they had started a camp game: how to have four people in a circle and not focus your eyes on any of them. Vi managed a laugh. Sin joined in. Trevor and Brandon chuckled.

Vi thought, I don't care about these people. Where's Jamie? Where's Marissa? Where are the people who count? Is this any way to spend Thanksgiving weekend?

Claudia's mother and Jonathan felt that Thanksgiving itself was a wonderful and satisfying tradition, but that the rest of the weekend left something to be desired. They hoped to start a tradition of giving a really spectacular party on the Saturday and had invited seventy-five people. Of course, some were to be away for the entire weekend, but most were delighted to have something scheduled for Saturday. Claudia's mother was determined to prove that she and her second husband gave even better parties than she and her first husband used to.

The house was frantic.

Jonathan was making the hors d'oeuvres, and the kitchen was a mess, although it smelled wonderful.

"What about Claudia's room?" she said. "It's disgusting in there. She hasn't picked up in about a year, and the junk is knee deep." This was not an exaggeration. Claudia did not have high standards.

"Just keep the door shut so nobody sees it," advised Jonathan. "Oh, I have to bring up the wine, almost forgot." He ran down to the cellar.

Claudia's mother switched on the vacuum cleaner to give the hall carpet another pass. She had had the house entirely redone after the divorce. While the old decor had been deep, intense navy blue, and hot dark gold, the new decor was creamy and soft and gentle. Most of the guests had not yet seen it, and she could hardly wait to hear their compliments.

The vacuum cleaner roared. Claudia's mother thought of the party. Jonathan chose wines. Neither of them heard the telephone.

Lynn's mother gave up after twelve rings.

Cathy's right hand had started shaking when she first saw Marissa, and it was still shaking long after Marissa had walked out of the room. It shook when Cathy held the hairbrush, and it shook when she rested the brush in her lap. Perhaps her hand represented her entire life and outlook. Shaky.

Marissa might just be in a bad mood. Or have a headache. Or Sin is waiting for her in the lobby. But probably, Marissa remembered all too clearly the summer months when Cathy had been mean and hateful.

I can't go to this reunion, thought Cathy. Did I seriously believe Marissa and Vi and Alicia would have forgotten anything and be ready to embrace me?

Cathy smoothed the green bedspread so no wrinkles showed to give a clue that she had ever been there. She walked out of the room, took the elevator downstairs, avoided the crush of incoming campers in the front lobby, and walked toward the back exit.

Trying to converse with Heather Anne's dear old friends was very heavy going. Nobody could think of anything to say. Finally Heather Anne suggested a nice ride in the countryside. Everybody leaped gratefully at this idea, and they all piled into the car. In November, after rain and before snow, no countryside is very pretty, but they pretended it was.

Lynn's mother called that house, too, to ask about the odd arrangement for Boston travel, but nobody answered the phone.

Cathy went out the back exit, where taxis were gathered. This exit, too, was glamorous and wide, but it had none of the vastness of the front lobby and none of the silver of the central light shaft. She was amazed to see a clutter of reporters, their cameras at the ready, their microphones up, all spread about the steps, yelling at some man getting out of a taxi. The reporters literally pinned the man to the taxi, shouting questions at him. There was a sick glee in their voices, as of hunters cornering a young fox. The air throbbed with their pleasure.

"You leave the house in order to make some kind of deal, Mr. Hesper?" shouted one reporter.

"What happened to the Ferrari collection, Mr. Hesper?"

"What's the real story about the Lake Placid property?"

"Who are you meeting here, Mr. Hesper? All dressed up for some special occasion? Is this another financial arrangement you're pulling off for your father?"

"What's that you're hiding under your coat, Mr. Hesper?"

It was Heath!

When she'd been at camp, Channing had written Cathy about the Hesper family scandals. She had been the first to identify "Dark" as Heath Hesper junior, and she had gone out of her way to taunt him more than once. Marissa knew, and Vi knew, and they hated her for that, too. Now she saw him, face set, eyes trying to look through the uplifted arms of the reporters to find a safe place, a passage into the hotel. He was as handsome as ever, but that oddly twisted smile he had—the campers used to say he'd had a stroke, as only half his face smiled at a time—had grown into a twisted frown now. He looked like a statue for unhappiness.

He looks, thought Cathy, the way I feel. She had not thought of Heath once during her own scandal. Typical, she said to herself. You are on the fringe, nearly untouched if you get right down to it, by your own bad judgment, and here is a guy whose father is destroying the whole family, a guy whose face has been changed in only three months by what he's been through—and you never even thought of him. Only of yourself.

Heath was wearing a handsome, black dinner jacket with satin lapels. He was clutching it together at the front as if his life depended on it. The reporters wanted to know what he was hiding beneath his jacket. Money? Maps to treasure? They laughed viciously.

But Cathy saw a tiny flash of yellow and red, and she thought—*it's the camp logo*. For a joke, he's wearing his Camp Men T-shirt with his dinner jacket. He can't let them know about the camp reunion or they'd come and spoil it for everybody. They must follow every member of Heath's family door-to-door. Oh, poor, poor Heath!

Heath tried to get back in the taxi, but the driver grinned. "I'm off duty now, kid."

The reporters laughed.

In a high clear voice, the sexiest one she possessed, Cathy said, "Gentlemen, kindly let me through. Mr. Hesper and I have a dinner date and you are making it quite impossible for us to reach the restaurant."

It was a very odd hour for a dinner date, but it was all she could think of on short notice. She tossed her hair. Her looks were elegant, even breathtaking; the wool of her deep crimson sheath was rich; and the gold of her hair, finer than jewels.

94

She extended a hand toward Heath, and the strangest expression came over his face. He was trying not to laugh. Good, thought Cathy. Probably the first time in weeks. I know the feeling.

The reporters began taking pictures of Cathy, which she enjoyed, and she postured for them, and gave them secret smiles. When somebody yelled, "Hey, honey, you getting any of that Hesper money?" she said, "My dear, I definitely have enough of my own."

The reporters followed them into the hotel. Cathy sashayed on, thinking—where do I take him from here? How do we escape?

Walking toward her was Pink.

So that's what it means to be trapped! thought Cathy, her heart missing beats, her knees turning to jelly. A photograph of me with Heath is one thing—but me with Pink? Never, never, never!

She jerked Heath's hand, and they dashed to the elevators, leaping into one just as the doors closed. They got out at the first stop, raced to the stairs, and ran on up to the fifth floor. Cathy got her key card into the slot on the first try, yanked open the door, and they jumped in, slamming it behind them.

"That was pretty neat," remarked Heath. "Just like a TV chase. A person would think you'd done this before."

Cathy burst into tears.

Heath looked as if he would have preferred a dozen hostile reporters any day. "I can't stand it," he said. "Don't do that, Cathy, please. Cathy don't cry. Come on, stop. Please?"

She did not stop.

She wasn't just crying, she was bawling.

Heath kissed her.

Another boy might have handed her a Kleenex, but Heath kissed her. It worked brilliantly. "I'm sorry," said Cathy, finding a Kleenex on her own. "It's just that so few people have had any use for me lately."

They sat on the double bed. The hotel gift basket tumbled into Heath's lap. "Smelling salts maybe?" he suggested, holding up a small bottle.

"No. That's toilet water."

"I've always thought that was a disgusting name for perfume," said Heath.

Cathy undid the stopper of the toilet water and sniffed it. It was very nice. She said, "Oh, Heath, I know you have enough troubles of your own, but can you stand to listen to mine?"

10

Sin Franklin seemed confused by the reunion, as if he had expected a different crowd entirely. The room filled. Every few minutes a little boy raced up to Sin to talk about how Sin had taught sailing and waterskiing. Kids popped up like empty bottles on a production line. Memories were poured in. Then they rolled down the conveyor belt for the next former counselor to cap them off.

All summer Vi had admired Sin. Thick blond hair like white sea foam against the golden wave of his tan, nose slathered in zinc, a whistle hanging on a lanyard around his neck. (The lanyard might be purple and white, or brown and blue, or pink and yellow; it was always the gift of a camper, handmade in arts and crafts, of narrow plastic ribbon you found only in camp, used only in camp, and for that matter, *liked* only in camp.)

And all summer Vi had restricted herself from

falling in love with Sin because Marissa worshipped him and, therefore, had a prior clearance, so to speak. Once Jamie had started seeing Vi, Vi forgot the very existence of the other boys, anyhow.

Now it seemed to Vi that Sin and the other boys didn't even *have* much existence. Nobody was saying anything worth repeating. They were babbling. Desperately making noise.

"Listen to us," said Vi. "We sound so stupid. We're trying to cover for something. What do you think it is?"

The boys were silenced.

Sin frowned and looked off toward the entrance.

Brandon took a handful of cheese sticks from a passing waiter.

Trevor shifted his feet nervously. "I think," he said unexpectedly, "it's because we're not official. When you're a counselor, you have a job and a place to stand. Little rules to follow, little people to guide, little cabins to fill. But now we're just hanging around."

Immediately for Vi, Trevor attained personality and was clearer in her vision than either Sin or Brandon, who acted as if this subject were vulgar and unwanted.

Trevor said, "I bet we'd all do better if we had on our T-shirts, like the invitation said. It would sort of tug us into camp. We aren't dressed for camp, and yet this *is* camp."

Vi loved to talk about clothing. (She had informed Charles on the opening day of camp, when he'd complained about the amount of clothing she'd brought, "But, Charles, life *is* clothing." This had not cemented her relationship with Charles.) Vi said now, "I know. I made a mistake in wearing this, anyway. My older sister really picked it out for herself." She looked down at the dark crumpled colors that swirled and blended and belonged on Jasmine. "I feel like the second act of a school play," she confided.

Trevor began laughing soundlessly, accompanied by a wide grin and shaking shoulders. "Vi, we're going to regret our analysis. Look to your left."

To her left the crowd had built considerably. Men and women who had attended camp twenty or thirty years ago. Little kids whose first two weeks away from home had been last summer. Dozens and dozens of them now filling up the formerly empty Mayflower Room.

And Charles . . . pushing a wheelbarrow.

A really truly wheelbarrow, with red wooden sides and a single fat front wheel and metal tips on the curved wooden handles. It was difficult to imagine Charles pushing this through the lobby of the Hilton, among the Gucci bags and the Samsonite luggage.

Stacked in the wheelbarrow were Camp Men T-shirts, years and years of old and new, faded and bright, extra large and children's small, like a history of Maine camp T-shirts.

"Put one on!" Charles was directing. "Doesn't matter what you're wearing. If you did not come in a T-shirt, this goes over what you've got on."

His first candidate was a plump middle-aged

woman who, the moment she tugged her extra large T-shirt over her designer sweater, looked positively obese; it gave her another twenty-five pounds. She and her companions giggled insanely, poking each other's latest, quickest weight gain. Before Vi's very eyes, they became the campers they had been many years ago, girlish and silly and happy with the latest dumb prank.

Vi studied her own layers, her belted loose shirt, her scarf and heavy rope necklaces. "Not me. If I wear a T-shirt over this, I'll look—"

"You'll look just like everybody else," said Charles firmly.

"A person goes to camp to become an individual," said Vi, trying not to accept a T-shirt.

"A person goes to camp to become an individual who can also function as part of a team," said Charles. "I never had any use for your shenanigans, Violet, and I won't take them now. Have a medium."

Vi snarled at her medium.

Trevor said, "Do you remember the time Vi and Marissa and Alicia came over to our side of the camp, Charles, and Vi thought there was a bat in her hair, and she screamed so loud all the boys came streaming out of dinner to rescue her?"

Charles groaned and moved on with his wheelbarrow, obviously shaken by memories of Violet.

"And how Vi was always telling horror stories to her girls at midnight," put in Brandon, "so we'd wake up to the sounds of murder in the girls' camp? And Charles would rush over, either rowing himself to death or driving the Jeep through the woods, and it was just the next episode of the Green-Eyed Maniac?"

Vi had been partial to stories in which a green-eyed maniac suffocated little campers by lowering the upper bunk on their faces.

"My boys always felt left out," said Trevor. "I never had any stories that good."

Vi was filled with joy. It was like laughing gas. Oh, the pleasure of being the center of attention! Vi wanted to stand there forever while they remembered her. She considered briefly telling a few stories about what *they* had done, but since she, Vi, was so much more interesting, it seemed a shame to break in.

"Games!" shouted Charles. "Time for games! We've got to get to know each other again, people! By the time this reunion is over, everybody here will be friends! Good friends! Whether they went to camp in nineteen eighty-eight or in nineteen fifty-eight!"

"Why would we want to be friends with somebody who went in fifty-eight?" asked Violet. "If I needed a friend that old, I could have brought my mother."

"Hush," said Alicia, following in Charles's tracks and trying to whip up enthusiasm. "And cooperate, Violet. You were always a thorn in Charles's side. Be charitable. The man is getting married in a few hours."

"Boy, you'd never know it," observed Vi. "He looks more like a guy who's going to hike the Appalachian Trail in a few hours."

"Don't suggest it," pleaded Alicia. "He probably would."

Alicia and Vi giggled, and Vi wanted to know what the honeymoon plans were. Vi loved to plan her own wedding. She liked planning her first apartment, too, and her first budget, and meals and furniture and job. She hoped to marry somebody without too many plans, as Vi had enough to go around and did not wish to compromise any.

"Exclusively four-star hotels in Paris, Rome, and London," said Alicia. "No tents, backpacks, or sneakers allowed."

Vi could only applaud this choice.

A big, overweight ex-camper from the fifties boomed out, "I guess camp fees are making you pretty financially successful, then, little lady, if you two can go gallivanting off to hotels in Paris all the time."

"One does not honeymoon all the time," said Alicia irritably.

"Some of us don't even date all the time," said Vi.

"You know what I remember?" said Sin, who found the topic of honeymoons entirely without merit and went back to camp memories. "That dance Cathy taught us."

Alicia and Vi rolled their eyes at each other. Camp memories of Cathy were not cherished by any of the girls.

On the other hand, they had all learned and loved the short dance Cathy had taught as a warm-up. It was a wild, rock-style body shake, to which you shouted a rhythmic cheer and twitched the appropriate muscles.

"So shake your ankles—two—three—four!" began Sin.

Immediately any camper who had been at camp the previous summer set down food and drinks anywhere and joined him in the second line.

> *"Your knees—two—three—four*
> *your hips—two—three—four."*

"I always liked the hip part best, didn't you?" Sin said.

Vi was busy getting ready to shake her tummy, but she took a moment to follow Sin's eyes. Just whose hips had he liked best?

In the entrance, framed by two, green plastic trees, stood Marissa.

I'm going to cry first, thought Vi. Then I'll run up to her, showering tears left and right.

She wanted to holler, the way they had in the dining hall at Camp Men. *You guys are late to dinner!! What did you do in that shower anyway—try to drown a seven-forty-seven?*

But Marissa looked the way Jasmine had tried to make Vi look. Elegant and older, calmer, and hardly even familiar. This was the girl who had arranged Ping-Pong relays in the water? Who had been the best horse in the pretend rodeo?

Vi took two steps toward Marissa and faltered.

Then Marissa saw Vi, and came bounding past chairs, campers, Pilgrims, even Sin, shouting, "Vi! Vi! Vi!"

The boys were forgotten.

The reunion was forgotten.

103

The Hilton, the waiters, the strangers, and the friends.

All were forgotten. Nobody existed for Marissa and Vi except each other.

Mercifully they were not aware that half the packed room had fallen silent to stare, filled with sadness and envy. For here was the reunion they had all come there to experience. A voice shouting across the room, calling out *your* name. Eyes misting with tears, hugs that would not stop but went on and on, as if squeezing friendship back into shape.

By now there were some two-hundred-fifty guests, the youngest eight; the oldest, seventy-nine. And all who could see Marissa and Vi paused and yearned. Nobody could hear what the girls said to each other, but they made up the dialogue in their minds.

How are you?

I'm fine, how are you?

Why didn't you write?

Because I'm such a dope.

It doesn't matter. I'm so glad to see you.

And I'm so glad you're here.

People had to turn away, for the real reunion they were seeing made their own seem empty.

Charles, however, did not deal in heavy-duty emotion. "Violet, you have not put your T-shirt on," he said angrily. "Hello, Marissa, good to see you. Put on a T-shirt, please. Think you can escape the rules as usual, Violet?"

Vi threw her arms around Charles, flinging her reunion love even his way. "Oh, no, Charles! I love rules. I absotively possilutely thrive on rules. Give me a T-shirt. Give me ten T-shirts. I'll wear one as a neckpiece and tie back my hair with another, and—"

"Vi, must you always do everything to excess?"

"Yes," said Vi firmly.

She and Marissa joined the boys, and the group of them laughed continually, staring at each other and at the other campers in their ridiculous T-shirts. Children in jeans and sweatshirts were bottled up in T-shirts two sizes too small. Counselors out of college who had come back to show off their success in the world (designer dresses and fine three-piece suits) now wore white T-shirts with suit and dress sleeves poking out and scarves and ties making peculiar chest lumps.

And then it all fell apart.

Cathy, slender and willowy, scarlet and gold, appeared in the entrance. She seemed strangely medieval, a portrait painted for a cathedral—her hair a precious metal.

And who appeared beside her, but Heath—dark and handsome in a black dinner jacket, black cummerbund, black shoes—and a Camp Men T-shirt peeking between the satin lapels of his jacket.

Marissa's joy at seeing Vi evaporated. She felt fat and ridiculous, the T-shirt twisted over her sweater, and her scarf bunched up beneath as if she had extra breasts. How could Heath be here with Cathy? He had lied to her! Pretending there was nobody else to talk to, and all along he'd been talking to Cathy. Probably dating her, too.

"Ghost rocks! Ghost rocks!" cried Charles,

climbing up on top of a table. "We're going to paint rocks, just as we always do every year on the last day of camp. Everybody will write a word or paint a symbol or initials that stand for his or her feelings toward Camp Menunkechogue and all the lovely, sunny, satisfying summers gone by."

The teenagers listened to this and ignored it. They weren't going to be caught painting pebbles at the Hilton. "I," said Violet, "am overcome by emotions. Hatred of Cathy. Pity for Alicia, marrying an idiot. Joy at seeing Marissa. Total humiliation at being caught in a T-shirt when Cathy looks like God."

Trevor said, "I don't think she looks like God. God would be more muscular. I think she looks like a Russian princess."

Marissa and Vi did not care for this comparison. "Why Russian?" said Marissa darkly.

"Because standing next to Heath, she's all mysterious like him, and different, like people whose era is ending. Who are going to be shot at dawn by the revolutionaries."

Vi giggled. "I like the part about them getting shot at dawn, Trevor."

Charles was lining people up, getting them ready to paint their rocks. He even had another wheelbarrow, full of rocks (real Maine rocks, no doubt, as opposed to substitute, measly old local rocks), and paint in primary colors waited in paper cups all down the length of long, paper-covered tables.

"I bet the Hilton management didn't know about these plans for painting when Charles rented the Mayflower Room," said Sin.

"I bet they don't know about it right now," said Vi. "I bet if we find the right manager quick enough, we can stop the whole humiliating thing in its tracks."

The campers Charles's age sighed and advanced very reluctantly to the tables, as if they would rather be dead. The small children vanished to safety zones, such as under other tables. Alicia, bustling around trying to work up enthusiasm, overheard Vi's plan.

"Don't do that," she pleaded. "He's so happy. Give this to him for your wedding present. Throw yourselves into this as if it's really camp."

But of course, it was not camp.

Nobody had come here, as they had to Maine, in order to do arts and crafts, or puddle in paint. Nobody wanted to flick color around the room and have green rocks appear.

If Vi had ever seen a party that was going to fail this was it. Not one person in the Mayflower Room was willing to pick up a paintbrush and paint. Two hundred and fifty totally unwilling campers stood very still. Charles galloped around, convinced that all it would take was a little friendly prodding. Alicia's hands knotted with worry that the reunion would not go right and, therefore, would spoil Charles's mood for the wedding.

Mother was right, thought Vi. Perhaps all mothers are always right. It was very very dumb to have a combination camp reunion and wedding.

"All right you guys!" yelled Vi. She descended on a group of kids she had never seen before in her life. "T-shirts—on!" she shouted. "Brushes—ready! Rocks—forward! And . . . *paint!*" With great faked zest she leaped into the painting of her rock, splashing red paint with an abandon that would give the Hilton management cardiac arrest. "I can't draw a straight line," somebody said, weakly trying to escape. "You can't draw a straight line, anyway," said Vi, "because the rocks curve." "I can't think of anything to write," said another weakling. "Start with the alphabet," said Vi. "A is for Alicia. B is for boats."

She was like a collie, nipping at the campers' heels. She dashed hither and yon, collecting painters who were trying to hide by the punch bowl, holding up finished rocks with gasps of admiration, and mixing more colors for people who were sick of red, blue, and yellow.

It worked.

People thronged to paint. Laughter started up again. T-shirts were flecked with paint. Opinions were delivered on final rock colors.

I am a leader, Vi thought. I figured I was just a kook with yellow hair who liked mascara more than hiking. But Charles only *told* them what to do. I got them to *do* it.

Her hair prickled.

Down with all elementary school teachers' reports!

Fie on all principals who said Vi was average.

Curses on the heads of Girl Scout troop leaders who told Vi she would never earn a badge.

I, Violet, am a leader.

Claudia, having found Roxanne and Dana on the balcony, stuck to them. In company she was safe from all the worries of the weekend. The three girls linked arms, and Claudia showed them every inch of the Hilton, with the result that they were quite late in getting to the reunion. Right off, they spotted Janey and Esther, and now they were five, practically an army, and began a clandestine war with a bunch of boys, paying no attention to the reunion Charles was organizing all around them.

The boys hid under the soda table. They were going to yank the cloth out from under the glasses and try not to spill anything. Claudia had once tried this herself. All you got was Coke on the floor.

She wanted to be far away when that happened. Abandoning Roxanne, Dana, Janey, and Esther, Claudia hurried to the opposite end of the room, where all the grown-up campers were painting ghost rocks.

She was second in line to paint when hair like a fluffy yellow duckling caught her eye.

"VIOLET!" screamed Claudia.

"Gosh, it's good to see you, Marissa," said Heath. He hugged her, squashy T-shirt and all. Then he held her away from him for a better look, and finally hugged her a second time, even harder. Just so had Alicia and Vi hugged Marissa.

So that's what a reunion hug is, she thought. A double dose. Assure yourself the person is real, stand back to study the face, and then the real hug. "Hi, Heath."

"I know, I know. You're mad at me. I don't blame you for hanging up the telephone on me. I deserved it."

He had not come with Cathy after all. They had

simply landed at the door together. Marissa forgave him everything, instantly.

"I was lying on the floor at the time," Heath went on, "and I had my feet up on the wall, which left perfect black prints from my shoes, and I was thinking how my mom was going to go crazy when she saw those black treads, and how mad you were because I was whining all the time."

If only I had known we were *both* lying on the floor with our feet up, thought Marissa. It would have made all the difference.

"Let me guess," said Brandon with a smirk. "You decided to clean up the treads and clean up your act and maybe even reform your father."

Marissa hated Brandon. She hated him with such ferocity that, when she whirled on Brandon, Heath caught her arm. "I can take care of myself, Marissa," he said very softly.

Marissa looked into Heath's face and fell in love with him. Great, she thought. Now I adore two of them. Sin *and* Heath. I have an infinite capacity to forgive, which probably means I will always love people who need a lot of forgiving. Which means I will be miserable forever. I should be in a loony bin.

She wondered what a loony bin might be. A big green garbage dumpster? The kind big enough to drive a car in? She could see all the girls crazy with love climbing in an orderly fashion into its horrid green maw, while the boys carelessly waved goodbye and found other girls.

"Love your hair like that," Heath added.
She looked like an escapee from that loony bin,

with the dumb T-shirt, but Heath did not see her clothes. He saw the girl who talked to him on the phone all those hard Monday nights.

Okay, adored one, thought Marissa, looking into Heath's eyes. Ask me out on a date.

There were a good many people between Claudia and Vi, plus a large table. Claudia showed no mercy. Black, white, old, young, fat, or thin, she shoved everybody out of her way. She hurled herself forward, only to find the table obstructing her path. She leaped on it, swung her feet over, and dropped on top of Vi, all the while screaming, "Vi, Vi, Vi, Vi, Vi!"

Older hands reached to catch the paint cups. They missed. Red, blue, green, yellow, and purple sloshed everywhere. Including on Vi's skirt.

Vi hardly noticed. I have been greeted with more noise than anybody else, she thought. My name has been shouted aloud the most. And I just found out I am a leader. So who needs Jamie?

With as much dignity as a person lying on the floor with a thirteen-year-old and five colors of paint on top of her can have, Vi said, "Hello there, Claudia. How have you been?"

They hugged in several colors.

"I knew you would do something like this!" shouted Charles. "Does anybody else spill paint? No, it's Vi. Always Vi! You'll probably do something to ruin the wedding, too, Violet. I know you, and your hot rollers and your curling irons!"

"Now, Charles," said a forty-year-old former

camper. "Let's mop it up. They're having a reunion. Isn't that what camp is all about?"

Charles sputtered and fumed while the woman grabbed a roll of paper towels and a pan of water and got to work. "I should have taken Vi's name off the computer list," he muttered.

Vi and Claudia picked themselves up. The Hilton would not be pleased. "You two go off now and get that skirt cleaned," advised the woman. "I'll clean this up. Charles, you hush."

Vi turned to run for the nearest water faucet, but first looked into the eyes of this pleasant middle-aged volunteer. Her face showed a sort of grief. She bent to cleaning as if she had needed an accident to happen, so she could busy herself with it. Had this woman come—all these years later—hoping to be remembered by friends and cabin-mates? And nobody had, or could?

Vi wanted to weep for her, but Claudia said, "Come on, Vi, we have to hurry before the stain sets. I'm really sorry about it."

"Don't be sorry," said Vi, running along with her. "I'm not sorry. All my life this will be the standard by which I measure reunions. Does anybody leap full speed over a barrier to see me?"

Nobody was talking to Cathy. Everybody had forgotten her. Instead of a golden dove to be cooed over, Cathy was a thin, unloved stranger. Her hungry eyes watched each reunion. Like the last child at nursery school to get picked up, her eyes said, *Where's my mother? Isn't she coming? Won't anybody come for me? Doesn't anybody want me?*

In an attempt to fit in, Cathy, too, had put on a T-shirt. Nobody teased her. She had stood alone to paint her rock. Nobody asked what her letters meant. Cathy had a soda, and nobody talked with her there. Heath had forgotten her. Sin (now that there was competition) was flirting much more genuinely with Marissa. Trevor's eyes followed Vi. As for Brandon, Cathy was afraid to get near him. If Brandon picked on Heath, he would certainly pick on her.

Marissa wondered what had brought Cathy. She had not liked camp. She had laughed at it. Nor had Cathy even liked any of them.

"Nice to see old Cathy getting what she deserves, huh?" said Brandon.

But it was not nice.

It was terrible.

For what on earth is more painful than a person without friends?

11

___

"First of all," said Vi, "I want to know why you were hugging Cathy like that at the top of the stairs."

She's jealous! thought Claudia. How wonderful. Claudia scrubbed at the red paint on Vi's skirt. "You'd better take it off."

Vi slithered out of her skirt. Jasmine's skirt, actually, she thought. To thine own self be true. If you are a ruffles and lace person, do not wear streamlined tailoring. "So?" she said to Claudia. "I'm waiting."

"I survived all September, October, and most of November without ever thinking of Cathy," admitted Claudia. "And if I *had* thought of her, they wouldn't have been nice thoughts. But you know what, Vi?"

The red paint came out completely. Vi wrung out the skirt. The only thing worse than wearing the wrong clothes to the reunion was wearing wet, wrinkled wrong clothes. "What?" she said.

"I think it doesn't matter what you shared over the summer as long as you shared anything. Good time or bad time. If you had it together, you're part of the whole memory. Cathy was a sharp, mean piece of camp, but she was the first person I saw here, so she made me feel glad."

Vi shook her skirt vigorously to try to unwrinkle it. She's wise, thought Vi. Claudia is thirteen, and she is wise. Perhaps it's all those remarriages. She wondered what Claudia would be like in years to come. Most likely she would never see Claudia again and would never know. It was an eerie thought—futures strung out like balls of string all over the world, and you could never follow any but your own.

Vi detested heavy thoughts. She shook this one off. "The weddings, Claudia. What did you wear, and did Heather Anne improve, and did Jonathan improve, and are you at peace yet?"

"How could anybody be at peace with two new stepparents?" said Claudia reasonably. "I'm at war, Vi. War." Claudia was taken with the word the moment she said it out loud, and she repeated it very softly to herself several times. War. That was it. They had won all the battles so far, but she was on new territory now. Okay, so she had had a little trouble on housing for the night. She was still going to win the war. She was not going to call home, whimpering, begging for help or money. They would have no occasion to laugh at her. She would sail through this weekend like an adult, and

116

saunter back through their front doors exactly when she felt like it, and not a minute before.

"Vi?" said Claudia. "I brought clothes to wear for the wedding. Can I change in your room?"

"Oh, sure. No problem. Great." Vi was flapping her skirt under the hot-air hand dryer.

Claudia thought Vi would probably let her sleep in her room, too. The carpets in this place were as thick as mattresses, anyhow. Claudia would take an extra pillow and blanket and sleep on the floor. That would show her parents. She didn't even want their crummy old beds. She had friends in this world who would let her sleep on their floor. So there.

Claudia was feeling cocky.

The bathroom door was flung open, and Janey, Esther, Dana, and Roxanne filled up all the floor space, hugging Vi, flapping her skirt for her, and telling her all they had done since camp drew to a close.

"Every Friday," confided Janey, "we have to give oral reports because we're taking speech this year. And every Friday, I am the hit of the class because I do another episode of the Green-Eyed Maniac. I get an A every time."

Vi was thrilled. She would have to tell Charles that she had, after all, given her cabin a skill to take home. So it wasn't swimming. We all had our gifts and telling horror stories was surely worthwhile.

"We have to give speeches, too," said Claudia, "but we can't tell stories. We have to do research and present information in an interesting yet captivating manner."

"How horrid," sympathized Vi. "The only thing worse than presenting information is pretending it's interesting."

They emerged from the bathroom just as Charles scurried past, apparently starting another fun-activity-for-Camp-Menunkechogue-returnees. "How can Alicia let Charles run around like that?" demanded Vi. "All hairy legs and a red-billed hat, like the center of a poisonous spider?"

Claudia giggled. "He's not that bad."

"I am making a vow," said Vi. "I shall never marry a man who runs around a Hilton hotel in his shorts."

"Vows, schmows," said Claudia. "Once they make up their minds to marry, they'll marry anything. Alligators, Communists, used coffee filters—people in love don't care."

"Wonderful ghost rocks, people!" cried Charles, beaming with pride. "I am so proud of the level of artistic ability demonstrated here today."

Now Charles had a large wicker basket, probably made twenty years ago in arts and crafts by a ten-year-old on the first day of basket-weaving. Lying in its messily woven center were hundreds of tiny red notebooks with microscopic printing on them:

Camp Menunkechogue Reunion

"You may not leave the Mayflower Room until you have at least twenty autographs!" shouted Charles. "This is to help you meet your fellow Camp Menunkechogue alumni!"

Marissa turned her thumb-sized notebook over

118

and over in her palm. "You can't even fit your thumbprint on this page, let alone a serious autograph."

"What is a serious autograph?" Heath wanted to know.

"More than a signature. A meaningful, thoughtful personal phrase or two."

"We'll have to read a lot of meaning into an X," said Sin, "because that's all there's room for. Give me a meaningful X, Marissa."

Vi, Claudia, and the three other girls joined them, and everybody grabbed an autograph book and began exchanging X's.

"But you haven't told us yet about Jamie," complained Claudia. "Are you dating every weekend? Does he call you every night? What's his excuse for not being here this afternoon? Have you gone to discotheques and McDonald's and Pizza Hut together so far?"

"He never called," said Vi, using Trevor's back for a desk and writing in print so small he would never be able to read it and thus she could not be embarrassed by it: *Actually it's you I love most, Trevor, ask me out please.* "I guess Jamie was just a creep after all," she added cheerfully. She wrote *Vi* with many flourishes all over her tiny sentence, to obliterate any possibility that Trevor could ever decipher it. It was nice to know that Jamie really was the creep, after all those weepy nights of figuring *she* must be the creep or he'd have called.

"So," said Brandon suddenly, and Vi was aware of his voice being loaded, like a shotgun, "what are the room arrangements? Who sleeps with whom?"

119

The way he said it made them all uncomfortable. Their accommodations no longer seemed like a more elegant rerun of camp—the boys' side of the hall instead of the boys' side of the lake—but a sleazy picture of people sneaking around in the dark.

"Four of us are in room five-twelve," said Marissa. "Vi and me and Cathy and a cousin of Alicia's named Brie."

"Brie?" repeated Claudia, giggling. "That's a cheese. Heather Anne is always serving Brie. It's mushy and disgusting, with leathery skin. Yuck. What kind of people would call their daughter after a cheese?"

"I can't help that," said Marissa. "It's the girl's name and she's our fourth."

Cathy edged up to the group.

"I know what you mean," Vi said to Claudia, ignoring Cathy. "I thought it was bad being named for a flower. But that's piffle compared to being named for a cheese."

They exchanged autograph books, X-ing pages all around. Heath stood with his hands jammed in his pockets. His jacket was flung back and the Camp logo rose and fell as he breathed. Marissa could not look at him and could not look away from him. She was almost twitching from the exhaustion of being so near him. "Marissa?" he said suddenly, softly. "Listen. All fall I've wanted you and me to get together, but I've been wiped out by what's happening to my family. I didn't have any energy for dating or anything. I'm sort of

120

moving into another stage now, if you know what I mean."

Marissa certainly hoped she knew what he meant. They stared at each other, and the stare was so intense she had to break it off, doing so with a toss of her thick hair. She stared at the floor and then quickly back up at Heath. He started to say something more—but Sin spoke first.

"I've X'ed your book, Marissa. And it's a very meaningful, profound X. You're going to love it." He handed her the book, and hung on to her hand when she accepted it.

Somebody take a photograph, thought Marissa. I have a boy whispering in each ear.

But Sin had ended whatever Heath might have said. They were back to tiny red autograph books, and exchanging pens and pencils. Claudia and Brandon and Trevor and Vi and Janey . . .

"Thirteen to go," remarked Cathy. "That's not a very good omen." She held out her own book rather desperately, for somebody else to seize and sign.

Marissa remembered a horrible story from high school a few years ago. A graduating senior had told her, "Nobody signed my yearbook. The day of signing, they were all busy signing each other's, and nobody remembered me. My book is blank." If Marissa had a blank yearbook, she would burn it. She wouldn't keep it to remind her she had no friends.

"That's true, Cathy," said Brandon, not taking her autograph book. "You haven't had very many good omens in your life lately, have you?"

There was something vicious in his voice that silenced them all—made them look back and forth between Cathy and Brandon.

"You know what, Cathy?" said Brandon. "I think everybody here just reads the front page of the newspapers. They figure the only scandal worth reading about is old Heath's dad ripping off old ladies' pension funds. But they haven't read the really interesting parts of the paper, have they, Cathy?"

Cathy was very still. Her fingers were knotted around a glass of Coke. She didn't look to anybody else to rescue her. Perhaps she knew they wouldn't.

Brandon said, "Why don't you tell them about your own juicy little criminal scandals, Cathy?"

Vi snatched Cathy's autograph book and began signing it. "Brandon, you make me sick. Whatever it is, stop it." She passed the book on to Marissa. "This is our reunion. Let's just remember the good things."

"And what good things can you remember about Cathy from last summer?" said Brandon.

Vi glared at him.

Cathy shivered, alone.

And Marissa thought of the good things from camp. Buddies. You always had to have a buddy, whether you were swimming or hiking or straightening the cabin. Buddies aren't just for safety, thought Marissa, or to make chores go quicker.

Marissa put an arm around Cathy, drawing her into the circle with Heath and herself and Sin, and shutting Brandon out. "She's our friend, Brandon. That's what we remember."

Heather Anne and Claudia's father got back from their drive in the country. The dear old friends had proved to be very silent old friends, and conversation had long ago run out. Claudia's father went into the kitchen to mix drinks. Piled on the bar was the stack of Claudia's schoolbooks.

Normally he hated going to the house where he had lived for fifteen years with his first wife, but just now he was glad to have an excuse to get away. He drove on over, only to find that Eve and Jonathan were giving a huge party, and there was no place to park. He drove around the block. He could not quite see himself walking in on all the people who used to be his friends, too, and now were only her friends. And if he went up to the door, probably Jonathan would be off talking to somebody and Eve would be in the kitchen and the door would be opened by a stranger. He'd have to ask if his ex-wife could please come to the door.

He could bring the books in the morning instead. But that was childish. They had had a perfectly civilized divorce; they were the best of friends now; there was no reason he couldn't just walk up, laughing at their daughter's forgetful ways, and deposit the books. He double-parked, gathered the books, and strode to the front door.

It was opened by Jonathan, who was astonished to see him.

"Hi," said Claudia's father.

"Uh—hello there. Come on, uh, in. We—"

"No, no. I just brought Claudia's schoolbooks. She forgot them, and I know she has a report on the Constitutional Convention due next week."

Jonathan looked at him oddly. "Claudia's with you for the weekend."

"No, she isn't. She's with you."

12

The party was noisy and successful. People were eating and drinking and laughing and telling funny stories. The music Eve had put on the CD player was just right, and everybody had told her how much more cheerful and open the house seemed in its new, light colors.

Claudia's mother and Jonathan and Claudia's father stood in the kitchen with the door closed, staring at each other. Claudia's mother was absolutely furious. It was all a plot on Claudia's part to ruin her evening. When she caught up with Claudia she would kill her.

Claudia's father thought that he and Heather Anne should not have to put up with this sort of immature behavior and that this time he wouldn't yell at his daughter, he would thrash her within an inch of her life.

Jonathan said, a little more coolly, "She's probably still at Lynn's, where she spent last night."

They sagged with relief. A simple answer, requiring no punishments, no worry, only a phone call. "Lynn's mother will be pretty annoyed with me, abandoning my daughter on her doorstep for so long," said Claudia's mother, laughing and dialing.

Brandon said, "You're willing to forgive anything, aren't you, Marissa? But some things can't be forgiven. Cathy here is a convicted drug pusher. Her boyfriend, Channing, got his stuff in South America. Cathy's on parole because Daddy has influence. Not unlike our old friend Heath, huh?"

Drugs? thought Marissa. At my camp? Among my campers?

"You're exaggerating, Brandon," said Heath. "Cathy was not charged and not tried, let alone convicted and on parole. The police agreed that she wasn't involved at all. It was Channing's operation."

"You believe that?" said Brandon scornfully.

Marissa turned to Cathy. "Did it touch camp?" she said fiercely. "Did all those little kids there for the summer—"

"No!" cried Cathy. "No, Marissa, I promise. Because—that's why I came this afternoon. Life has been so awful. And camp was—camp was good."

Good. The word settled among them.

Heath folded his arms and stood behind their barrier. Why was camp good, he wondered. Because it was broken down into two-week sessions? Did goodness require organizing, like camp?

126

Camp was good to me, too, he thought. But normal life entered in. School, grades, teams, family, TV. Attending my father's trial. Is good still possible when all *that* is around?

Vi produced Kleenex for Cathy, and they all managed to laugh a little, and finish up their autograph books. The scene had given them an immense appetite. They attacked the refreshments with laughter and shouting.

Brandon left.

How mysterious, thought Marissa. Another one with a secret life I will never understand. He'd been boring, a nobody, at camp. He'd come here— for what? To be mean to Heath and to be sure we were all mean to Cathy? What is *his* story? What made him so mad?

But she would never know. Their paths would never cross again, and if they did, Marissa would avoid Brandon.

"You have enough sour cream on that potato chip to open your own delicatessen," remarked Sin. "So you're Cathy's best friend now, huh?"

Marissa flushed. "You can't be mean on a day when everything's supposed to be good."

So that's it, thought Heath. You schedule *good*. Maybe I need to schedule Marissa. Learn more about it. He helped himself to some Doritos, thinking about next weekend. Maybe Marissa could come into New York, and they could . . .

"So," said Sin, being friendly, not taunting like Brandon, "I understand your American history class is pretty grim these days. Teacher likes to talk about ethics while staring at you, Heath."

Heath froze. He had told nobody about that. Nobody but Marissa.

Sin added helpfully, "Marissa phones me after your Monday night calls. We talk about you a lot."

Claudia's mother put the phone down very gently, as if she were afraid of something. "Claudia told them she was visiting her aunt Gertrude in Boston. She took a train by herself this morning, supposedly to Boston, but it was a local. Lynn's mother tried to phone each of us, but nobody answered."

The men looked blank. "Aunt who?"

"Boston?"

"What does that mean?"

"I think it means that Claudia has run away from home," said her mother.

Charles produced a banjo. They sang "I Love to Go a-Wandering," and "O Susannah," and their own camp versions of "Clementine" and "Sipping Cider Through a Straw."

"And now," said Charles, "it is time to repeat the camp pledge." He stood reverently. Alicia had long ago left to get her hair done, and he was alone, ridiculous in his shorts and cap, bony knees and pale skin.

The kids jabbed each other with sharp elbows to keep from laughing at him.

> I promise to be a friend
> to people around me and to the earth.
> I promise to love the world
> and all her glories.

*I promise to encourage, to praise, and
to be patient.
To let the world know
I am a Camp Menunkechogue . . .*

The last word of the pledge was an unintelligible chorus of "girl" and "boy."

Cathy started crying again.

Heath tried to think of one single glorious thing in his life and couldn't. He could not look at Marissa. She had betrayed him to Sinclair Franklin.

Vi added another promise. To go on being a brilliant leader.

And the reunion was over.

The lines broke up, the hugs changed texture, becoming good-byes instead of hellos. Final photographs were snapped. Everybody hurried toward the exits, as if vacuum cleaners and maids were coming in on the other side and they didn't want to get caught.

Everybody seemed to know something Cathy didn't, as if they were operating on an urgent schedule she hadn't received a copy of. Or perhaps she was just out of energy. For weeks she had run on nerves, and the first act of kindness toward her, instead of restoring her strength had sapped her. She tottered while the others gamboled.

She yearned to get up to their shared room. The boys would go to their own room, the girls would wiggle out of these silly dumb T-shirts (although Cathy felt an affection so deep, she probably would save the T-shirt the way she saved yearbooks: with love, forever) and have girl talks. She and Vi and Marissa could be friends now.

Cathy did not even feel on trial. The sick horrid feeling that you will have only one chance was gone. Long talk, thought Cathy contentedly, and pleasant stories, and interrupting each other with better ones, and ordering pizza at midnight. "You know what?" she said suddenly. "Laury and Dana aren't here."

"I know," said Vi. "Isn't it odd? Laury and Dana were my triumphs. They really and truly did become better people from going to camp. And they didn't want to be at our reunion."

Cathy thought about this. Of course they might have had to go to the doctor, or visit their grandmothers, or do school projects. But probably not. "It's terrible to face people who had a hand in improving you," she told Vi. "But those two loved you, Vi, so I thought they'd come to say so."

Vi looked quickly to see how much sarcasm there was in Cathy, but she seemed to be entirely straight. What on earth were Cathy's camp memories? What "good" was she referring to that she had found in camp? Certainly not her own.

Of course, memory is silent.

Invisible.

Known only to you.

And mostly, you have to pull memory out. It doesn't arrive without permission. You can leave it alone, or let it surface.

She wondered what Jamie remembered. He was like Daniel Boone when he flexed his muscles. All the little boys wanted to grow up to be just like him. How, wondered Vi, could Jamie not want to spend a single Saturday afternoon with all his admirers?

"Honestly," said Marissa to Vi as they reached the lobby, and Sin and Heath went off in a different direction to their own room. "Boys."

"I know just what you mean."

"The only one I'm sure of is Brandon. *Species vomitus.*"

"So true. Write him off. But what about the others?"

"I don't know. Listen, did you read our horoscopes today by any chance?"

"No. Let's buy a paper."

"I want them both," said Marissa, and she did not mean both newspapers.

"Of course," agreed Vi. "And I have decided on Trevor. Which is interesting, because I'd forgotten he was alive. I won't tell him that, of course. It isn't terribly flattering. I think he would be excellent for the school's winter dance. That's in only two weeks. I've got to have at least two dates with him before I can ask him to take me to the winter dance, which means both dates have to be next weekend."

They bought a paper, ignored the headlines, and flipped, giggling, through the pages, stopping briefly at Ann Landers and the comics, and reading out loud their horoscopes.

"Wait, wait!" cried Claudia. All the girls her own age were leaving, and she had gotten lost in their camera-clicking and good-byes till next summer. She dashed to catch up to the older girls. She could not wait for the evening. It would be such fun! Nobody was funnier than Vi, anyhow, and Marissa would be there, and Cathy was turning out not to be so bad, and they would make jokes about old Brie being a cheese, and talk about the wedding. It would be the best slumber party that Claudia had ever been at. Better than camp even.

And my parents won't even know where I am, she gloated.

Claudia turned in her luggage ticket and got her ocean-liner-sized suitcase. But Vi wouldn't notice. Vi had brought four of these to camp. Claudia lurched into the up elevator with them, shoving her suitcase against an innocent person's ankles. Marissa was reading Sagittarius. "What's Taurus?" asked the woman with the damaged ankles. "Read me Taurus." So Marissa read her Taurus and was still reading it aloud as the girls got off on the fifth floor. Taurus never did hear the end of her horoscope.

"What are we going to do?" said Claudia's mother, beginning to cry.

"Now, now," said Jonathan. "She's got a good head on her shoulders. Let's not panic."

"Not panic? My thirteen-year-old daughter takes off for Boston, stopping to change trains in New Haven, and you don't want me to panic? What about people who prey on little girls? What about drugs, and rape, and prostitutes, and all the other horrible things?"

A guest came into the kitchen. "We're out of ice! Got any more? Shall I—" The guest broke off and looked at the trio.

"I'll get it," mumbled Claudia's mother, stumbling forward, knocking an empty dip bowl to the floor, and opening the refrigerator instead of the freezer. The guest fled the kitchen as soon as possible.

"We'll call the police," said Claudia's father. He was shaking. His baby girl. Alone. At night. Mad at the world, and her parents—what stupid, dangerous decisions might she make?

"We'll have to telephone all her friends. See if she told them anything," whispered Claudia's mother. "Oh, God, we'll have to admit to the whole world that our daughter ran away. Can you imagine what they'll say about divorced families then. I can hear the words *broken family* at every dinner table in town."

We did break her family, thought Claudia's father. And I have put Heather Anne first, and Eve has put Jonathan first. "We'll worry about her reasons for running away later," he said. "Right now, we have to do something constructive."

Cathy tagged along, too exhausted to contribute, just floating in the girl talk and feeling pretty good. She and Marissa had the same birth sign, which was nice, but she was too tired to tell Marissa the coincidence.

Just as they unlocked the room door, Brie appeared. They all had to introduce themselves. Brie had an appropriate name after all, for she was cheesy-looking—pale and bloated. Vi and Marissa and Cathy, and especially Claudia, carefully did not look at each other for fear of laughing out loud.

"I am utterly exhausted!" cried Vi, racing around the room with enough energy to win a footrace.

She opened her suitcase, hung up a dress, peeled off her T-shirt, and whipped out her hair dryer and hot rollers and makeup. "Oh, the emotional turmoil of it all!" she said. "I get the bathroom first. I am too tired to wait for anybody."

"You can't have the bathroom first, I'm already in here," said Marissa, closing the door on them.

Violet plugged in her hot rollers to preheat.

Brie opened the closet door and removed a long plastic bag in which hung a peach-colored formal gown, with satin sash, and ivory lace. From a shoe box she withdrew matching satin slippers. For the first time, Cathy saw, lying on Brie's side of the double bed, not the hotel's basket of hand lotion, and toilet water, and shoe polish cloth, but an old-fashioned bouquet of chrysanthemums, ferns, baby's breath, and lace.

Lace? thought Cathy.

Vi and Marissa shrieked when they saw the gown, abandoned bathroom and hot rollers, and held up the long dress, crying, "Put it on! Oh, it's beautiful! You'll look so pretty. Oh, Brie, I'm so jealous!"

"But what's it for?" said Cathy.

"The wedding," said Vi and Marissa, too absorbed by the gown to glance her way.

"What wedding?" said Cathy.

13

———

"I can't believe there's a party in my living room when I'm trying to find my daughter," said Claudia's mother. "Who are all those laughing people? Why don't they go home? I feel like going out there and shooting them all."

Jonathan hastily said that he would run out and play host, leaving Claudia's parents to deal with the missing child.

"Well, we've telephoned every single girl we can think of that Claudia is friends with, and either she didn't tell anybody anything, or they're being very loyal." Claudia's mother had been crying for over an hour. Her face was splotchy and swollen; her eye makeup, dark glops where she kept wiping at her eyes with tissues.

The police had said that, since Claudia had gotten on a train and left the state, all they could do was call the New Haven and the Boston police to look for her. They sounded bored, as though thirteen-year-old girls did this all the time.

The phone rang. "Yes, yes?" cried Claudia's mother, and then made a disgusted face. "It's Heather Anne, for you."

He had completely forgotten Heather Anne and the dear old friends. He told her everything quickly, before she got any madder at him.

"What do you want me to do?" said Heather Anne simply.

"Stay there. She might phone there."

In the room at the Hilton the girls jostled for mirror space.

"Claudia," said Vi in a strangled voice. "What— what are you putting on?"

Claudia stared at Vi. "My bridesmaid's dress." She looked down with pleasure at all the frills and ruffles, and twisted herself a little so the satin would whisper.

"Claudia, you can't wear that. You're a guest this time."

Claudia looked at the older girls. They were looking back with amusement and pity. Oh, they were trying not to, but they were laughing at her. I've worn the wrong thing! thought Claudia, completely demoralized, unable to look at any of them now.

Vi said kindly, "What else do you have, Claudia? A dressy dress? Or even a skirt and blouse?"

"Just my jeans and my sweatshirt." Why was it so demoralizing to be dressed wrong? It was only cloth, and yet the wrong cloth at the wrong time, and you'd rather be dead.

"Well, she can't go in that," said Marissa irritably, as if Claudia were offending her.

"Here," said Cathy. She wriggled out of her beautiful red wool sheath. Vi bundled the bridesmaid's dress back into Claudia's suitcase, and Cathy tugged her dress over Claudia's head. "But you're so tall," said Claudia, "and that dress is so long. It'll reach to the floor."

It nearly did. Vi tossed Cathy a belt, and Cathy secured it around Claudia's skinny waist. Then Cathy began hitching at the dress, pulling it up toward Claudia's chest. When the hem was the right length, she adjusted the top of the dress so it drooped down over the belt. Suddenly Claudia was wearing a sophisticated blouson dress that looked just right.

Claudia stared at herself in the mirror. If I had asked Heather Anne what to wear, she thought suddenly, I wouldn't have gotten it wrong like this. And they wouldn't have laughed.

"Dry your tears," said Cathy. "Hurry up. You need some makeup."

"Hey," protested Vi. "I do makeup around here."

They all began to laugh, remembering Vi at Camp Men. Cathy put on a white terry robe.

Claudia suddenly realized that Cathy was the only one not ready to go. "But, Cathy," she said. "What are you going to wear?"

Cathy shrugged. "I wasn't invited."

Heather Anne set down the telephone. She was suddenly horribly afraid. It was very dark out.

Very cold. Boston? What had made Claudia choose Boston?

She walked back into her living room and said unsteadily to her visitors, "I'm terribly sorry. My stepdaughter has disappeared. Probably run away. We—we don't know what we're going to do. They're having a conference at the other house."

How stilted it was to say "the other house."

I was mean, thought Heather Anne. Oh, I pretended to be nice. Fixing up her room. But I knew she hated coleslaw.

The dear old friends said they didn't mind, they would run along home, maybe get a hamburger along the way, not to worry about them.

Heather Anne had not been worrying about them. Pushing them out the door, she could hardly remember their names. She sat by her phone, wishing she could be with the others at the other house, in on the worrying and working. She wished Claudia would telephone *her* for help instead of *them*.

They were gone.

Cathy folded and refolded her T-shirt.

She closed the heavy drapes. The green room was as dark as a forest at night.

She could hardly tag along with them to the wedding. You couldn't decide that the hostess had done a lousy job with the invitation list and change it on your own. Certainly not a wedding and reception. Certainly not when Cathy had flirted with Charles over the summer, and had even made a little headway, and Alicia reasonably enough hated her forever.

How amazing that, downstairs, the kids had stuck up for her. Abandoned Brandon instead.

But Cathy thought that none of them were really her friends—not Marissa, nor Heath, nor Vi, nor any of them. They were the camp pledge. *A friend to people around me and to the earth.*

Generic friends, thought Cathy.

Like generic toothpaste, or generic spaghetti-o's.

If she turned on the television, it would be surrender. *I have no friends, but the boob tube will light up when I press the button. At least I can hold hands with the remote controls, and join in the laughter that came from a tape.*

I have to do something, thought Cathy.

She did not feel despair, and she did not feel contentment; she was in a holding position, and it was certainly better than the position she'd been in the last few months. The girls would be back after midnight, probably, and she would listen to them, and be on the fringe of their talk, and that would be better than nothing.

She resolved to go downstairs to one of the many restaurants in the hotel and eat supper by herself. Marissa and Vi and Brie would have a late supper at the wedding reception. Everybody in the restaurant would be a stranger. Doing things alone was easy when you didn't know anybody. The fear was that somebody you *knew* would see you alone, and say, Ah-hah! Nobody wants to be with Cathy; I could have told her that; I don't want to be with her, either.

She put on the clothing she had planned to wear in the morning. A long, tight jeans skirt with a kick pleat, a very large man's shirt in faded checks over a navy turtleneck, and a bright scarf and gold belt. I look like the back-to-school spread in *Seventeen*, she thought.

She decided on the Country Squire Café. Tables along one wall were meant for single diners, and there were half a dozen business people, men and women, sitting by themselves, reading newspapers or thrillers. She was almost hidden in her corner, what with the row of diners and the hanging plants.

Pink walked in with two men. He carried a briefcase. Each of his companions carried briefcases. Whatever else Pink might be, he was not an executive with a briefcase full of important papers.

Rage came in bright hot colors.

It was like lying on her back in the sand at the beach, the sun piercing her closed eyelids and setting off hot white flares in her head.

She hated Channing and Pink.

She hated them for their own ugliness, their own crimes, their own disregard of humanity. She hated them for dragging her into their sordid business, without even telling her. She hated them for using her and laughing at her and setting her up. She hated knowing that she had been just on dates, and the police and her parents and Brandon all thought she should have been gathering up evidence and drawing conclusions and stopping all drug traffic on her own between movies, maybe, or over strawberry sundaes.

Skunks! thought Cathy, staring at Pink.

She wanted to smash the little red candle-glass. Rip the menu to shreds and stab Pink with both her forks. She wanted to grab the pot of coffee a waiter was carrying and pour it in Pink's lap.

"Take your order, miss?" said her waiter cheerfully. He was a nice-looking young man, a little thin and tired, as if a long day promised only to get longer.

"An old boyfriend of mine just walked in," said Cathy. "He's the last person on earth I want to have see me. I don't suppose there's a way I can sneak out of here?"

The waiter grinned. "I don't think somebody with your looks can sneak anywhere," he said. "But I'll take you through the kitchen if you want."

She had made his day. He loved standing between her and the boyfriend. He loved shepherding her past the ovens and the deep fryer and the startled short-order cooks.

"Thanks," said Cathy.

"Hey, no problem. Always wanted to rescue a girl."

Strangers could be so nice. Impulsively Cathy gave him a kiss and ran on out into the hall. He probably wanted a tip more than a kiss, she thought. Oh, well. I was in a kissing mood.

She did not know if Pink had spotted her leaving the café or not. She had not wanted to turn her head and risk showing her face.

I wish there was something to do to stop rotten Pink, thought Cathy. I didn't know what was going on before. But now I know. What can I do? What can I manage—without getting smeared again myself?

. . . Marissa thought that when she got married, she would choose a room with windows. All the flickering candles in the world could not replace daylight. There was something dreadful about starting your married life in the half-light. Marissa wanted the blessing of sunshine for her wedding. She approved of the flowers, though: huge exuberant bouquets of chrysanthemums in every autumn hue—crimson, wine, and gold— shot through with color and joy and vibrance.

. . . Violet thought that when she married, she would have even fewer candles. Oh, the romance of dusk! So cozy, even in a big impersonal hotel room. The old-fashioned scent of the narrow white tapers wrapped the marriage with love. Vi disapproved of the flowers. Too gaudy. Vi would have only the most delicate of flowers at her wedding, and the palest of pastels.

. . . Claudia thought that if *she* had to get married someday (not likely, considering her views) she would skip all this wedding-ceremony junk. Oh, sure, it was nice to have a pretty gown, but Claudia would rather have dresses she could wear again, lots and lots of them, closets full of them, instead of one single white dress that had to stay in a plastic bag for the next fifty years.

"Dah dum da dummmm," sang Claudia.

Heath and Sin kicked Claudia.

Claudia snickered.

Marissa said, "I break bones, you know."

Trevor said to Vi, "Are you going to the reception?"

"Of course I am."

"Want to dance with me?"

"Of course I do."

"Are you a good dancer?"

"Of course I am." Vi gave him her pixie smile, full of mischief and delight. Trevor puffed out a long, slow lungful of air. The hair on his forehead danced.

Vi considered her next move thoughtfully and then put her hand in Trevor's.

Trevor considered her hand with equal thoughtfulness and then wrapped his free hand around hers.

Vi was just planning her next move—a slight, but definite, squeeze—when the wedding march began, and the guests got to their feet and turned to face the rear.

But instead of Alicia's cousins in peach satin, a huge, bearlike body suddenly galumphed down the *center* aisle—not one of the side aisles, like a late guest should—and shoved in among them, stage-whispering, "I can't believe I'm so late! My God, I used to lead compass hikes in the Maine woods, and I couldn't find my way to the Hilton. Can you believe it? Listen, how are you, Vi? Hey, Sin! Heath! Can't believe you showed up! Trevor! Guys! Great to see you all."

Vi felt fully responsible. Had she not prayed to the Lord God, to all writers of horoscopes, thrown coins in fountains, and wished on the first star that Jamie would show up?

Jamie leaned around Trevor, squeezed betwee
Claudia and Vi, and planted a kiss on Vi's cheek
The kiss was noisy and smoochy and Jamie re
mained twisted over, grinning like an insane orth
odontist's model.

"Ssssh," said Marissa fiercely.

"I have to say hi, don't I?" said Jamie.

"Trying to steal the show from a bride," re
marked Claudia. "You should meet Heather Anne
She's your type. Pushy. Worthless."

"Shut up!" hissed Vi.

The music, luckily, was loud, and the aisle long
and one could hope the wedding party had no
heard and had barely seen Jamie's arrival.

Brie walked slowly past, transformed by he
pleasure and her gown from a stolid cheesy gir
into a beautiful happy cousin. A very small frienc
of Alicia's and a very tall friend of Alicia's walkec
past, holding identical bouquets, both trying
neither to smile nor cry.

There was a pause. The music strengthened
And Alicia appeared.

Alicia had no father and walked between her
two brothers. Alicia was utterly beautiful, with her
dark smooth hair and her ivory skin, her bright red
cheeks, like a painted doll's, and her breathtaking
ly beautiful gown.

But mostly, Alicia was smug.

Vi bit her lips to keep from laughing. Alicia made
no attempt to disguise the fact that in the great
hunt of life, she was the lioness of the day. Alicia
was preening herself every foot of the aisle.

As for Charles—who ran mountain expeditions

and taught waterskiing, who could cope with bed-wetting campers or the cook quitting on Parents' Day—Charles was scared. He did not look as if he would be able to utter a syllable, let alone vows.

"It's a good sign," Claudia informed them. "It means he's thought about what he's getting into. People like Jonathan and Heather Anne, they just spit out the vows like slogans for washing machine detergent. You know *they* aren't going to be there for richer or poorer."

"I don't want to be there for poorer, either," whispered Vi.

"Me, neither," said Trevor. "Let's get married for money."

They all sssshed each other, and tried not to laugh or talk once the organ music ceased.

But Heath thought, My mother married for money. And where is she now? All the money on the East Coast was ours for a while, and it wasn't worth it and never will be.

Heath thought about marriage.

The minister spoke of how married couples must deal together with the trials and tribulations of life.

Trials, thought Heath.

What does anybody here but me know of trials?

14

Vi remembered a day in camp when Jamie, out on the playing fields after the flag had been lowered and the last song sung, had picked her up and swung her twice in a circle before kissing her. All the campers had been in awe. That was love—being swung around.

Charles stumbled through his pledge to Alicia. Alicia sailed through hers. After the minister's pronouncement, the recessional began.

Vi thought: Being swung around isn't love. It's just somebody with muscles showing off.

The bridal party almost ran back up the aisle, the guests began snapping photographs, and the music got louder and louder. The room ceased to be a sacred place for vows and became a party, with everyone who couldn't reach their friends just shoving chairs out of their way to make paths.

Jamie made a fist and punched Heath lightly.

"Say, I keep reading about you guys," he said. "So how's it going, Heath? Huh? You hanging in there?"

"Sure am," said Heath, punching him right back, but not so lightly. "How about you, Jamie? Having a good year?"

"Oh, yeah, sure am, yup, didn't get on the football team, couldn't stick to those rules, you know? I mean, you'd think it was prison the way they expect you to get lots of sleep and never touch booze and keep your grades above a C."

Marissa stared first at Jamie and then at Vi. "Was Jamie always like this? I don't remember him being so stupid. He was always this terrific jock, out there mowing lawns and repairing roofs and canoes or being Daniel Boone for the little kids."

"We didn't talk that much," admitted Vi.

The boys all changed character, so they could greet Jamie exactly as he greeted them—loudly, with a lot of swearing and hitting.

"Did the summer Jamie turn into a different, less decent winter Jamie?" said Marissa. "Or did we make up the summer Jamie, and this was the guy all along?"

"Who cares?" said Vi. "I prefer to wonder why we didn't fall passionately in love with Trevor, who is a doll."

"Because Trevor was passionately in love with Cathy, remember?"

"It's coming back to me. Speaking of Cathy, Marissa. What about the reception? She'll be alone in that room for hours and hours and hours while we're down here dancing and eating."

"I know. I've been worrying about her since we left."

"It's a real burden being a nice person," remarked Vi. Acknowledging that she and Marissa were nice, however, took away a lot of Vi's worry about Cathy in the first place.

"Next year," said Marissa, "my resolution is to be mean and happy."

Heath had left his wedding present in his room. He slipped away to get it before going on downstairs to the Riverboat Lounge, where the reception was being held. At the elevators, a reporter caught his arm. "Why, it's Heath Hesper junior, isn't it?" said the reporter, smiling.

"Don't you guys have anything better to do than wait for me?" said Heath.

"Lots of stuff. I came here to interview a Japanese businessman about the economy and cover a meeting between a former terrorist and a current senator."

"Don't let me keep you."

"Well, as long as we've bumped into each other, I'd like to ask you a few questions about your father's plans."

Heath tried to circle the reporter, but the man just stepped alongside, so that they did a queer little dance right on past the elevators.

I'm reaching my limit, thought Heath. I'm going to deck one of these guys, even though I promise my mother every single morning not to antagonize the press.

Heath's fist, which had been aching to hit somebody since Jamie had barged into the wedding, doubled up again.

"I had a few minutes to spare," said the reporter, "and when I found out you were really here for this camp reunion, I kind of had a friend look into this camp of yours. Helps to have a rich father, doesn't it?"

"I was a counselor," said Heath through gritted teeth. "I didn't pay anybody. I got paid. And I earned it."

The reporter smiled. "So did Charles Crandall. Kept us reporters away from you, didn't he? Kept the TV news out, didn't he? Probably worth the Jeep and the minivan your father gave him to keep you out of view, huh, kid?"

Heath was moved beyond violence into shock. There *had* been a new Jeep and a new minivan at the camp. All the returning counselors had teased Charles for actually spending money on mechanical objects for a change. *Getting rich now, huh?* they had teased Charles.

That's my price, thought Heath. Or Charles's price.

A Jeep and a minivan.

Cathy thought camp was good. Well, it wasn't. It was just one more place where people were out for themselves.

Heath didn't know what to do. Going to the reception and speaking to Charles was out of the question. Going home was worse. Going alone to his room was impossible. Phoning Marissa, his favorite good-spirits technique, would not work.

Heath stood next to the reporter, like a victim waiting to be mugged.

Claudia was taking bets on how long this marriage would last. "Ten years?" she said. "Do I hear ten years? That's how long they last these days."

"Claudia, don't be sick," said Violet. "If we were at Camp Men right now, I would throw you off the cliff."

"Your mother agrees with me," Claudia pointed out.

"I'll throw her off, too."

"That's a lot sicker than betting on divorce," Claudia said.

"Claudia, just try to be a person," Vi commanded. "We are going to the reception, we are not taking bets on divorce at the wedding reception, do you hear me? Marissa breaks bones, remember? Do you want to go home in an ambulance?"

Trevor was laughing his head off. "I like your style, Vi. I don't know why I never did anything about it during the summer."

"You were in love with Cathy over the summer."

"I know." Trevor shook his head wonderingly, as if such thickness on his part was impossible to imagine in these clearer days.

Jamie bounded around having his own noisy, pushy reunion hours late. He was totally unselfconscious and completely unaware that everybody was hoping he would drop dead.

"*You* were in love with *Jamie* over the summer,"

Trevor said, in a voice that implied Vi's choice was far worse than his.

"I know. What can I say? Youth."

Claudia's parents attacked her room, hoping for a clue. She kept no diary, no date book. Mostly they found a lot of dirty laundry. Claudia's mother piled it in the hall, trying to get to the bottom.

"We sure won't find anything important on the floor," observed Claudia's father. "I don't think it's been visible since last year."

The phone extension in Claudia's room rang, and he seized it. It was Lynn's mother. "Lynn and I have gone over and over their conversations last night," she said. "You don't think—oh, I hate to suggest this—it sounds so crazy—but Claudia really loved camp, she was always telling us about it. You don't think she could really be heading for Maine, do you? Back to camp?"

Cathy marched across the lobby, trying to think of some way that she could get Pink. Oh, there had to be something she could do to the man! She paced past Reception and the ranks of elevators.

And there stood Heath—bones intact, upright position, but apparently in a coma. A reporter was asking him questions he did not even hear, let alone answer.

A reporter! thought Cathy. Reporters have their uses. They've used me and they've used Heath. Why should I not use one of them? She said, "Excuse me, Heath, you don't mind if I take your reporter for a minute, do you?"

Heath scarcely reacted.

"I have a *real* story for you," Cathy informed the reporter. "I know you like crime or you wouldn't be bothering Heath. Now I have a live, current, up-to-the-minute crime for you, as opposed to old, boring, last year's crime. And you have a camera. There's a drug deal going down right now in the Country Squire café. The man you want is the one two tables from the back on the left, with abnormally flushed cheeks . . ."

The reporter listened to Cathy's saga. "If you're setting me up," he said threateningly.

"Then you can come after me. Just don't reveal your source to Pink when you interrogate him."

The reporter was insulted. "I would never do that."

"You'd do anything," said Heath.

The reporter grinned. "Okay. I'll check it out."

He left, and Cathy pushed Heath into the first up-elevator. "Come on," she said. "We'll go to my room and call room service. Are you all right? You look ill."

"*Cherry Ames, Psychiatric Nurse*," said Heath. "I never would have thought it of you, Cathy."

She giggled, breathless with her coup. She would sleep well tonight. She just hoped the reporter was good at his job. "Heath, I am improving. I can feel it. Character is growing away, inside me, taking root."

"Growing? Like in third grade, when you used to tell each other that if you swallowed a peach pit it would grow in your stomach?"

"Yes! I am turning into a good person, Heath."

"Siccing a reporter onto somebody is good?"

"It is if the person is bad."

Heath said, "This is too deep for me. I have to show up at this rotten reception for a minute, I guess, get rid of my gift, and then I'm going home."

"Rotten! What's rotten? Heath, they're all wonderful. Of course you want to go to the reception. Marissa adores you, and Charles and Alicia and—"

"Marissa told Sin every secret I told her. And Charles accepted a bribe in order to protect my privacy last summer."

Cathy was silenced.

They got out on the fifth floor and walked to Cathy's room. She opened the door with her key card, and Heath walked to the window, jerked the heavy drapes open, and stared out into the dark. "I guess I should thank you for the second rescue of the day, Cathy. It was good seeing you again, I hope you sort your life out—and I have to be going."

"Heath, please stay and share my french fries. Please?"

"Look, Cathy. I'm not hungry. I don't want to talk. I'm not going to ask you out, so don't flirt. Don't butter me up. Give me a rest, huh? I didn't ask you to barge in and I don't owe you anything."

Cathy glared at him. Did Marissa really want to take this husk of a person, stuff it back full of humanity, and try to prop it up? Yes, probably Marissa did. She loved a challenge. Cathy hoped that Sin would ask Marissa out first, though. Sin would be so much more fun.

"Listen," said Cathy. "I used to be ninety-nine percent bad and one percent good. Right now I'm striving for fifty-fifty."

"Aim high," said Heath sarcastically.

"But Marissa is ninety-nine percent good and one percent bad. You have to have a little bad in you or you're not human. Give her another chance. You need somebody you can count on, Heath."

"I can't count on anybody."

"Yes, you can. Let's go to the reception together. I bet Charles can explain the Jeep, and Marissa will be glad to see you."

"Sure, he can lie away the Jeep, and yes, Marissa will be glad to see me. Big deal. I just want to—to—"

"Hide," said Cathy.

Heath's fists tightened again. He had to remind himself that socking girls was not in his line.

"Let's not hide, Heath," she begged. "Let's play it's camp. I wasn't much of a camper. I wouldn't join in, or work hard, or help anybody. But camp enriched us all, Heath. Let's go to the reception. Come on."

"You weren't invited."

"So I'm crashing it. If you're right, Charles isn't a perfect person, either. Taking free Jeeps. What's a couple of hors d'oeuvres without permission compared to that?"

Claudia's parents started working through the stacks of paperback books, old school notebooks, treasures, old letters, and cassette tapes. Claudia had a Camp Menunkechogue address book somewhere that would have phone numbers in it.

"Can you remember Vi's last name?" said Claudia's mother. "She was always telling me Vi was perfect. Maybe she went to Vi. Or called her. Or Vi would have a clue."

"I just can't believe she'd go to Maine. It's November. They probably have a foot of snow on the ground up there, and the camp would be completely boarded up. You can probably only get there with a snowmobile, anyhow."

"Oh, David, I don't know whether I want to hug Claudia a million times or kill her. How can she put us through this?" cried her mother.

He sighed. "I guess her argument would be that we've put her through a lot and we deserve it."

It was Heather Anne, attacking Claudia's other bedroom, who found the address book. She called Violet's house, and talked to her mother, and then phoned the other house. "There's a camp reunion this weekend," she said to Claudia's father, who answered the phone. "Violet's there now. It's at that new Hilton up the shoreline. Claudia probably told Lynn about Boston to make her jealous. I imagine she's eating hot dogs right now, telling those horror stories Vi taught her, and showing off her sweatshirt."

Claudia's mother was so relieved she could hardly stand. "I knew it," she said to her ex-husband. "I'm going to kill Claudia. No. You go get her and kill her for me."

15

_____

Alicia was so excited and full of energy she could not bear to sit down, certainly not to eat roast beef, which is a heavy meal, and requires concentration and sharp knives. Alicia commanded the band to play—anything, as long as it was loud—and forced Charles to dance.

Vi thought the marriage was not off to a good start when one partner had to be forced to dance. But Claudia said it was off to an excellent start, because that same partner was willing to sacrifice, and look foolish in front of hundreds of people, being a totally inept dancer.

"He looks nice in that," said Vi dreamily, for even Charles was handsome when dressed for his own wedding.

Trevor said, "Come on, stop staring, let's dance."

Vi beamed at him. "There are probably only two

boys in New York State who actually love danc
ing," she said, "and I'm with one of them! Wha
luck!"

"Luck?" said Trevor. "*Luck*, Violet?" He swung
her out in front of people, and now the dress tha
Jasmine had picked was the right one, for the skir
was full and it danced by itself, spinning aroun
her legs. "I am a true camper, you know," Trevo
told her. "Always prepared. Got a Swiss Army
knife with everything on it but a magnifying
glass."

"Oh?" said Vi. She was aware of eyes on them. I
was good to be the center of the action. She knew
people were smiling. Trevor wasn't clumsy like
Charles. Trevor was excellent. They were excellen
together. It was going to be an excellent night.

"But I needed a magnifying glass, see, so I found
an even truer camper. Charles. His Swiss Army
knife, of course, has a magnifying glass."

"He's carrying a Swiss Army knife on his wed
ding day? The man is sick."

Trevor said, "So guess what I magnified?"

"What?" Vi took his hand and leaned back hard
into the rhythm of the rock music, and their bodies
rushed up close again, and parted with strength.
"Oh, no," she said, realizing what had needed
magnification. "You didn't?"

"Yes, I did."

Vi swung around and danced with her back to
him for a few beats. "Oh, well," she said, swinging
back, pretending the blush was from dancing.
"Now you know. It was supposed to be a secret."

"What's the point of liking somebody if you keep

158

it a secret?" Trevor wanted to know. "I mean, you won't get very far that way."

When their bodies parted for some really violent footwork, a waiter carrying the first course passed between them. Soup. Trevor and Vi did not need any discussion to agree that dancing was better than soup any day.

As far as Claudia was concerned, the waiters could unserve the first course anytime. Probably had vegetables in it, soup usually did. If Claudia ever did get married, and was forced to invite people to a reception, she would serve food that people actually liked. Twinkies and Mallomars. Oreos and Reese's Peanut Butter Cups. Coke and Mountain Dew.

Alicia danced out of her new husband's arms and into the embrace of the best man. Charles danced with his mother, and Brie danced with an usher. Now Sin was dancing with Marissa, and now with Alicia. Marissa danced with Charles, and Vi worked her way through the line of handsome young ushers.

Claudia thought, I am the only one not dancing.

But, then, she was very nearly the only one there under sixteen. I personally am the young-camper-invite, she thought.

The music slowed, and the girls lowered their heads onto the boys' shoulders. The waiters cleared the untouched soup.

Claudia wondered what it felt like to dance. How did you know, the way Vi did, when to fling yourself about and when to rest on your partner's shoulder?

She wondered why the room was called the Riverboat Lounge. Except for three small circular windows with brass fittings, there was nothing remotely shiplike about it. The Hilton must have been very happy when Charles came to book his space. He was probably using more of the Hilton than IBM was.

Marissa's happy feet stumbled to a stop. For the second time that day, she stared at the couple appearing in the door. Heath and Cathy. Arm in arm.

Vi and her partner—an usher—stopped next to Marissa. "Just when you forgive a person," Vi said.

Marissa nodded grimly. "They sin again."

"Did I hear my name?" cried Sin. He was stuck with Brie and gladly let himself be diverted off the dance floor into a conversation with the girls.

Marissa pointed to the door.

"Oh, *that* kind of sin," said Sin.

"Well, we all half wanted to rescue Cathy," Vi reminded Marissa. Vi managed to leave her usher and attached herself to Trevor again. Trevor grinned. "Heath just acted on it."

Half wanted, thought Marissa.

"Oops!" cried Vi, "here comes Jamie, got to run, come on, Trevor, may I have this dance?" She and Trevor fled rather rhythmically. Sin put his hand on Marissa's waist.

Oh, why do I always yearn for the one I *don't* have? thought Marissa.

* * *

"There," muttered Heath, spotting the group just as Vi and Trevor danced away. "Now, listen, Cathy. Alicia's over there hugging some relatives, and Charles is at the bar with his bachelor friends. If we're quick, they won't even see us. We'll just slip right down there where everybody else is and blend in."

"We don't want to be quick," said Cathy. "We want to confront Charles and demand an explanation."

"Speak for yourself," said Heath. "I have had enough confrontations."

Cathy, to his horror, strode purposefully through the crowd of dancers, waiters, and guests toward the bar. Heath looked quickly around for rescue, but Marissa was dancing with Sin, and Vi was dancing with Trevor. There, in front of him, however, stood skinny little Claudia, staring wistfully at the beautiful teenagers and bridesmaids and ushers.

Claudia was the happiest person at the party. She was probably even happier than Alicia. Alicia *knew* she was going to be the center of attention, but Claudia had never expected such a thing. "I'm only thirteen, Heath," she protested.

"So what? I'm only seventeen."

Claudia found that neither of them could really dance, but that it didn't really matter. There were two of them, and they were moving to the music, and that was joy. "You're all right, Heath," she complimented.

"I don't even know why I'm here. When the music stops I have to leave."

"No! Please don't! When the music stops, dance with Marissa next."

"What is this," said Heath, "National Get-Heath-a-Girl Week?"

"No, it's camp reunion. Besides, you came late and you missed the announcement. You have to dance with everybody. Charles said so, and you're not allowed to leave until every woman here has been your partner."

This sounded so like Charles that Heath actually believed Claudia, and glanced around appalled at the number of women, their ages, and their waistlines.

Claudia giggled triumphantly. "You believed me."

"I thought you were trustworthy."

"Nobody's trustworthy," said Claudia. "Haven't you learned that yet?"

And Charles was between them, one hand high up on Heath's wide shoulder, one hand low down on Claudia's thin little shoulder. "*I* am trustworthy," said Charles. "Haven't you learned *that* yet?"

Claudia was embarrassed and giggled too loudly.

Heath swallowed, looking sick and angry, and looked away.

"Yes, I have a new Jeep," said Charles. "And a new minivan. Do you really believe your father bought them for me? Heath, I am truly insulted. You applied as a counselor. Your name meant nothing to me. In fact, I forgot your real name because Vi nicknamed you Dark the moment you rrived. I bought that Jeep from a friend who had o move away. And I got a good deal on the ninivan through the local dealership. It involved a rade: the dealer gets to hunt on my land in the winter. Your father had nothing to do with any of t. I've never even spoken to the man. A TV crew lid come to the camp to interview you, and Alicia sent them off. And that's it."

Claudia's father and Heather Anne drove to the Hilton. "Now that it's over," he confided, "I'm nore mad at myself than at Claudia. I think she nay even have told us about this reunion and we didn't bother to listen."

"At least she's all right. When I was sitting there alone with the silent telephone, every time the house creaked, I thought of another terrible thing that could have happened to her."

They parked in the underground lot, came up in an elevator, and emerged in the sleek lobby. It was bustling with people. "What room is the Camp Menunkechogue reunion in?" Claudia's father asked at the desk.

"It was in the Mayflower Room, sir, but it ended hours ago. The room was cleared by six. And it's"—the desk clerk glanced at her watch—"ten-thirty now."

They were stunned. Claudia was *still* missing? "Could she be registered here for the night?" asked Heather Anne.

Claudia's father checked, but there was no Claudia Goodman registered. "Can you remember

her?" asked Claudia's father desperately. "She wa
wearing a camp sweatshirt."

"Sir, I'm so sorry, there were dozens of girls an
boys in camp sweatshirts."

David and Heather Anne stood in the hustle an
noise of the lobby. People brushed past them
telephones rang, elevator doors opened.

Could Claudia have gone home with somebody
thought her father. Is she really running away afte
all? Is she so mad at us that—

He wet his lips and tried to think. Running
business was so much easier than bringing up
daughter. He and Heather Anne looked for th
telephones, finding some down the hall that led t
the Country Squire Café. "Eve?" he said frantically
"She may have been here, but the reunion ende
over four and a half hours ago. What do you thin
we should do now?"

Vi's head was completely full of Trevor. She ha
danced with him almost every dance, and whe
they were forced to dance with other people, wha
with wedding etiquette, he waved at her. I'm i
love, I'm in love, I'm in love! she thought. I knew
would happen one day. And it happened righ
here. At my reunion.

Reunion.

The word meant repeats. But for Vi, it was a
new. Being in love with Trevor, and him being i
love back, was new. Being friends with Cathy wa
new. Being the leader of the ghost rocks was new
She had never before attended a wedding for
marriage she was sure was going to last foreve

and never before had she spent a night at a really magnificent hotel.

Marissa whirled by, dancing with Heath.

I did have a repeat, thought Vi. Marissa. We are going to be friends again, I know it. I will make sure of it. I'm not scared the way I was, scared of calling her, or of writing to her. Scared she didn't really want me to.

Her thoughts tumbled around, glowing, like hot dry clothes in a dryer, and she felt wonderful, and her head was resting on Trevor's shoulder, and she could dance forever like this, with no interruptions.

"Vi?" said Claudia.

Trevor stopped dancing. Vi wanted to keep going. I'm not your counselor now! thought Vi. Can't you see I'm very very busy? But she said, "Hi, Claudia."

"Listen, I really have to talk to you about something. It's a decision I'm making and I need your advice."

Vi sighed. "Okay. I'm listening."

Claudia looked meaningfully at Trevor. "It's private," she said.

I may kill you, thought Vi. This is not camp! This is life. Don't tell Trevor to leave.

Trevor said, "Okay, okay. I'll dance with the bride for a while." He grinned and threaded through the crowd. Vi watched him go. What a fine personality and a great mind and a terrific body he had. How could she not have noticed this over the summer? Where had her brain been? What had she been doing to miss Trevor?

"Vi?" said Claudia.

Vi remembered. She had been spending every waking minute with Claudia, and Janey, and Laury, and Dana.

"Let's go up to the hotel room," said Claudia. "We'll be very private there. And by the way, I can spend the night there, can't I? Sleeping on the floor? I won't be in the way, I promise."

Vi said, "Spend the night? Aren't your parents coming for you?"

"Well, that's what I have to talk to you about."

Claudia tried to pull Vi with her out of the reception, but Vi resisted. She kept looking for Trevor, but he had disappeared from view. Vi tilted back and forth, searching. Claudia asked her twice to come, and Vi barely heard.

Claudia gave up, and left alone.

That's three couples in one day who would rather not be with me, she thought. Mommy and Jonathan. Daddy and Heather Anne. Vi and Trevor. They all have better things to do.

Claudia wanted to sob for a couple of years, and break something big, like a house.

Vi would let her stay, but it would not be the wonderful slumber party Claudia had had in mind. She would be in the way. They would all want to talk about their boyfriends. Not about Claudia.

She had never felt so lonely.

It had been a strange day—wonderful parts when she was in control, and brave—and terrible parts when she was collapsing and unwanted. Claudia's feet slowed and she dragged herself toward the elevators.

"Okay, okay," said Vi, panting. "I'm here! You took off without me. Now start talking. What's going on?"

Claudia ignored her.

"Claudia, you can't get into the room without me. I'm the one with the key. Wait up."

Claudia waited. And there, across the lobby, going in the opposite direction, was Heather Anne. Headed for the Country Squire Café.

Those horrible rotten parents! They couldn't even come themselves. They had found out where she was and sent Heather Anne. Claudia could not imagine how they had located her. It made her feel like such a baby—having the perfect secret weekend away from home—and her parents just drove up. Only it was not her parents. They, of course, had important things to do. Parties to give. Heather Anne was good enough to drive over at night and fetch annoying old Claudia.

"Who's that?" asked Violet.

"Heather Anne. My stepmother. Oh, there's nothing I hate more than all of them getting along like camp buddies. Telephoning each other like sisters. Substituting for each other and carpooling. I hate them all."

Vi stared after the vanishing Heather Anne. "She looks just like me."

"I know. I hate her."

"Claudia!"

"I can't help it if she has hair like yours, Vi, and wears frilly clothes like you. She isn't you. Now if *you* had married Daddy, it would be different."

It certainly would be. Vi considered this novel

thought: herself as stepmother. She blinked, and returned to dreams of Trevor.

Claudia shoved Vi into the elevator and viciously punched the up button. "That does it, I'm really running away now."

"You are?"

"Yes. I just have to get my coat. I'll fix them. They'll never find me now. If they had stayed home the way they were supposed to, I'd have gone home myself. But no, they had to send Heather Anne." Claudia made it sound like a disease. She leaped out on the fifth floor, and dragged Vi into the girls' room. She ripped off Vi's belt and yanked off Cathy's dress. She tore open her suitcase and jerked out her jeans and sweatshirt and old sneakers.

Vi did not know what to make of all this violence. "What are you talking about?"

"And you don't care, either!" shouted Claudia, turning on her in a fury. "Well, I'm sick of it. If nobody cares, then I don't care!" This did not make sense, and Claudia knew it, and that only made things worse. She was crying now, too, and the tears made it hard to see the laces on her sneakers.

The desk clerk tapped on the glass wall of the phone booth that Claudia's father was using. "Sir? There was also a wedding. A Camp Menunke-chogue wedding and reception. In the Riverboat Lounge. Perhaps your daughter is there."

A camp wedding.

How bizarre.

Claudia's father could not imagine what a camp

168

wedding might be. "Thank you!" he said fervently, and he and Heather Anne rushed to the Riverboat Lounge.

"Hi," said Trevor, ready to knock on the door to room 512 just as Claudia flung herself out. Claudia's thick sneaker sole crushed Trevor's toes, but she didn't say she was sorry. She raced down the hall toward the stairs. Trevor stared after her. "Vi, I thought you were just going to talk for a minute, but you left the party completely. Is something wrong? What's—"

Vi grabbed his hand and jerked him on down the hall after Claudia. "Hi, Trevor, I'm glad you came. Claudia! Claudia! Wait up! What are we talking about?"

Claudia flung open the fire door and pelted down the stairs. Vi dropped Trevor's hand, apparently feeling she could make better time without him, and tore after Claudia. Trevor got the fire door in his face, but recovered, skidded around it, and yelled down the stairwell, "What are you doing?"

"Running away!" shouted Claudia, her voice echoing up the long long shaft.

"From what?" he shouted back.

The girls were getting away from him. He had wasted time asking questions. Oh, well, thought Trevor, might as well follow through on this. It was hard to get up any real speed going down a set of stairs; all you could do was trot down each riser. Claudia, though, was going like a bat out of hell. Vi was yelling for Claudia to slow down and explain.

Claudia was yelling that she was through, through, through!

Trevor caught up to them a few steps before the lobby door. Claudia flung the door open. She and Vi burst out together. Trevor got the door in his face again, sidestepped, and leaped out, crashing into Vi, who had finally stopped running.

There in the lobby stood a crowd of assorted wedding guests, hotel guests, and employees. In front of them were Alicia, resplendent in her wedding gown, and Charles, red with rage and screaming.

"I knew it!" yelled Charles. "I knew you would do something, Vi. If it wasn't electric curlers and screaming at night, it was Mallomars and cheese Doritos! I knew you would start something at my wedding. You talked Claudia into running away from home. I'll never have you for a counselor again, Violet. I'll never give you a reference. I'm not even keeping your wedding present!"

16

"Okay, okay," said Charles, finally, after about a dozen different explanations. "So I jumped to conclusions. I'm sorry, Vi. A person does that around you."

Vi sniffed.

"Okay, okay," said Charles again. "I'll order pizza for everybody staying over at the hotel. Will you forgive me then? Pizza with everything for everybody?"

"As long as it doesn't have anchovies," agreed Vi.

Alicia's mother was storming around at the back of the crowd. "I told you nothing good would come of having a combination camp reunion and wedding. Runaway thirteen-year-olds, berserk fathers, Charles in a fit, that girl, Vi, throwing her shoes at him, that boy, Trevor, jumping between them to save Vi, and some reporter who's lurking around catching drug dealers photographing it all."

"Now, Mother," said Alicia, who rather liked the idea of being a front-page photograph in a newspaper, "I think it all went very well. Nobody will ever forget my wedding. And Claudia got the reunion she needed most—with her own father. And Vi and Trevor fell in love, at my very own wedding."

"Hmph," said Alicia's mother. "I think you should leave for your honeymoon before something else happens."

Alicia thought this was a very good idea.

Almost too fast for throwing confetti, it was over. Reunion and wedding had ended. Bride and groom had gone. First cousins and second cousins had retired for a postreception reunion of their own. The lobby was empty. Camp Menunkechogue boys and girls of any age had left.

Claudia sat wedged between her father and her stepmother in the front seat of her father's sports car. A wonderful thing had happened. She had not had to tell her father how rotten he was; he'd said it himself. He apologized a hundred times, insisted that he loved her, and even thought that it was all his own fault that she didn't have a ride home from the camp reunion. He figured she had told him and he'd just forgotten. Heather Anne had said she was sorry, too, and had promised never to serve coleslaw and to let Claudia redecorate her bedroom any way she liked. Then they had telephoned Claudia's mother from the hotel and her own mother wept. Her mother did not mention her ruined party or Jonathan. Just cried with relief that Claudia was safe.

This is how things should be, thought Claudia. I am the center of attention, and they are going to do things my way.

They drove through the centers of three towns. Christmas lights had been put on, and late at night the cities glittered and twinkled and sparkled.

"Daddy?"

"Yes, honey."

"I didn't tell you about the camp reunion," Claudia confessed. "I was going to run away for two days and see if you even noticed."

Her father winced. Claudia steadied the steering wheel. "Oh, Claudia, that makes it even worse. *See if we even noticed?*"

"But you did notice." Claudia smiled happily. "Everybody noticed." She remembered with pleasure the final scene, with people hugging and weeping and shouting accusations. Vi had even tried to throw things. Claudia loved it when people threw things.

"Claudia," said her father, "your mother and I promise to notice a lot more often. Okay?"

She patted his knee. She did not know where her own anger had gone, but it was nice to be without it. A year was a long long time to be furious. She felt rather light, and giddy, as if she had not eaten for days.

"How was the reunion?" asked Heather Anne.

"It was nice," said Claudia. "I think I'll go to camp again next summer after all."

* * *

Since the girls' room was the largest, they had the pizzas delivered there. Heath, Sin, Trevor, Cathy, Vi, and Marissa sat in a circle on the floor and ate hot pizza. Brie was still with her cousins. Mozzarella cheese strings ran from fingers to pizza boxes. Cathy treated them twice to more Coke from room service.

"I was thinking all day what different memories we each have of camp," said Vi. "There's nothing else that is silent and invisible like memory. You can see what schoolbooks people are carrying, and what instrument for band, and what coat they sling over their shoulders. But you never see someone else's memories. Even if you shared the same experience."

"Hey, she's a philosophy professor," kidded Sin.

But Trevor said, "I can think of something else that's silent and invisible."

"What?"

"Love," he said softly, then ruined the romantic thought by immediately stuffing a whole wedge of pizza into his mouth and smiling around it: a clown's face of tomato sauce and mushrooms.

"I have no use for love if it's silent," remarked Vi. "I like a love that comes right out and says, What are you doing Saturday night?"

The boys chewed pizza vigorously. First Cathy, and then Marissa, and, finally, Vi began laughing at them. The boys looked embarrassed, but determined to eat pizza rather than answer that remark. "They'll run out of pizza soon," said Cathy. "Then they'll have to answer." She was the odd one out.

174

Trevor would ask Vi, and both Heath and Sin would ask Marissa. But Cathy was neither sad nor hurt.

I am among friends, she thought. Friends because of camp. I don't know if they are lasting friends. But I have what I prayed for this morning. And I know I can be nice. I still want to be glamorous. I can't help it. It's fun to be a regular girl, wearing a jeans skirt and chomping down pizza. But I want to be a shining golden star. I still have to work that out. But I can, I know I can.

She said suddenly, "May I tell you about Channing and the drugs?"

They all squirmed uncomfortably.

She said, "It was glamorous. Not the drugs, but dating Channing. He had a lot of money, and we were always off somewhere being glamorous. I loved it. I never wondered how he got all that money, and I never wondered who all those people were giving those parties. I was wrong. I should have paid attention. I should have thought. But I didn't know about the drugs. I didn't even see them. I was just busy showing off."

They were not looking at her. Eating pizza suddenly had become quite a task, requiring a lot of thought and staring down at the wedges.

"So I'm trying to learn not to show off so much," she said. "Be a person and all. This is sort of my—well—my trial run. My first lap."

She waited.

And Marissa said, "You dressed Claudia. That was a good start."

175

"And rescued me," said Heath. "Twice. That was pretty fair."

Marissa set her pizza down. "Heath, I told your secrets on you and I'm sorry. Of course, it was just to Sin, but still—"

"Just!" squawked Sin. "I was a very important security leak, Marissa. I mattered!"

Heath said to Marissa, "It's okay. Sin—he's a good friend, too. I guess it wasn't so much gossip, as friend to friend. I—uh—have a hard time with friendship now and then." He flushed and reached for another slice of pizza. But they had eaten it all. He grabbed a napkin instead and crushed it.

Vi flung herself back on the carpet, her fluffy hair half an inch from Trevor's lap. "We're going to get weepy and worthless if we keep this up. It's because we're afraid we'll never meet again. It's now or never for confessions. So I am going to bring things back to the level of pizza and Coke. Everybody come to my house next Saturday. I'll rent a good movie. Do you think there's an Abbott-and-Costello-Go-to-Camp movie?"

"If there isn't," said Heath, "we could make one next summer."

"Heath! Would you actually go back and be a counselor again next summer?" cried Vi.

"Well, Marissa's going back."

He didn't add anything else. But the rest did their own adding. Marissa looked as smug and happy as Alicia had looked coming down that aisle. Cathy and Vi giggled. Trevor said he would bring the Coke. Marissa said she would bring a salad.

"Salad?" moaned Sin. "You mean we have to

176

have something nutritious? I am against nutrition."

Their talk went on and on, into the small hours of the morning. Brie never did show up. She must have found better company among all those distant relatives and twice-removed cousins.

Finally, awkwardly, the boys left.

There were no kisses, nothing but teasing, no good nights and no good-byes. The boys just backed out into the hall and then they were gone.

Cathy thought, there's another silent and invisible thing—friendship. And they gave it to me tonight.

She knew why there had been no good-byes. First, because Vi had given them all a second chance. Second, because they didn't know how to have a good-bye that was meaningful enough for all that had happened, both last summer and tonight—and yet not commit them to anything— like real dating. She turned to look at Vi and Marissa and knew that the foreverfriends needed to be alone.

She did another nice thing. She dropped her hopes for more girl talk and said she had to wash her hair and all, she'd be in the shower for ages, she hoped they didn't mind.

Vi slipped out of her clothes. Her figure was not a whole lot different from those of the twelve-year-old campers she had supervised. Very slowly, enjoying the slippery richness of the fabric, Vi slid Jasmine's ivory silk gown over her head and arms and shook herself lightly to make it fall the rest of the way. It was too long, and lay on the floor as if she lacked feet.

Marissa had forgotten about the realities of spending the night. She had omitted to pack nightgown or pajamas. She had even forgotten her toothbrush and toothpaste. That was what happened when you were sick with love for Sin and sick with guilt over Heath. You couldn't remember your toothpaste.

One good thing, she thought. I am over my crush on Sin. How sad, setting aside a crush that had never amounted to anything.

Violet handed over Jasmine's peignoir. "Wear this to sleep in."

Marissa put on the robe. She was taller than Jasmine, and had a lovely, curvy figure. She fastened the tiny satin-covered buttons, grateful that she slept on her back. All those bumps would be very unpleasant to lie on. Tiny ribbons circled the neckline like satin rivers, and broke into dozens of tiny bows at the bustline. Two panels of lace fell to the floor and met more rivers of ribbon.

Marissa ran her fingers through her hair so the long, thick dark curls fell against the gleaming robe. She stared at herself in the full-length mirror. This is how I will look on my wedding night, she thought.

Marissa had always seen herself as stern and sturdy, but now she was soft and romantic and infinitely desirable. She wondered to whom she would be married? Heath? Sin? Or a boy she would not even meet for years?

"How come you never wrote?" said Marissa.

"I'm not very good at letters."

"Yes, but it was *me*."

"Well, you didn't write to me, either. Or telephone."

We were each hurt, thought Marissa. We each expected the other one to go first. Why was that? "I guess I was afraid," she said slowly. "That you'd say you had better things to do. Or better friends."

"Well, I don't," said Vi, and they burst into tears and hugged one more time, and the tears were like cement—they were foreverfriends again. They told each other about school, and boys, and guessed about what might happen at Vi's next Saturday, and whether Sin's feelings were hurt, and if Claudia would be fine now, and how amazing that Cathy had turned out to have nice qualities after all.

There was a knock on the door.

They thought it was Brie, at last, and opened the door without looking through the peephole.

But it wasn't Brie. It was Sin, Trevor, and Heath.

Vi, a fragile mermaid in the long gown, and Marissa in her lace and ribbons stared at them.

"Wow," said Heath.

"Do we have to go back out?" said Trevor. "Or can we just stand and stare?"

"I could get my camera," offered Sin. "I figured you two wore Camp Men T-shirts to bed."

"We'd have come back sooner if we'd known this was going on," added Trevor.

"Nothing is going on," said Marissa. She felt naked. Ridiculous when nothing showed but her hands. All summer they had seen her in a bathing suit and she hadn't felt naked then. "Why did you come back?" she said.

The boys shuffled around and looked embarrassed. Why, they're sort of afraid of us! thought Marissa. We're glamorous. I bet they were going to take the plunge and ask us out—and now—

She was very glad there was to be another party. The boys might cut and run, but now she and Vi would have another chance. She made a mental note to dress without threats on Saturday—jeans and a shirt.

"Well, it's a good thing you showed up and you're still dressed," said Vi. "Go down to the little store near the newsstand in the back lobby and buy Marissa a toothbrush and toothpaste."

"You go," said Sin to Heath and Trevor. "I'll stay here and entertain everybody."

Heath just smiled. At Marissa. Her heart flopped over. "My treat," said Heath. "I never sent you flowers. Never bought you a great record or a new cassette. Let me get you toothpaste."

They all laughed.

And Marissa thought that she had loved camp, and she had loved this reunion—but next Saturday at Vi's.

That would be a time for loving.

ABOUT THE AUTHOR

Caroline B. Cooney is the award-winning author of several novels for young adults, including *The Face on the Milk Carton, Family Reunion, Among Friends, The Girl Who Invented Romance, I'm Not Your Other Half* and *Don't Blame the Music*. She lives in Westbrook, Connecticut.

STARFIRE

Intelligent Fiction For Teens.

NEWS ON GREAT BOOKS FROM BANTAM.

EXCITING NEWS!

Loveletters—the hot-off-the-press newsletter.
Now you can be the first to know:

What's Coming Up:
* Exciting offers
* New romance series on the way

What's Going Down:
* The latest gossip about the SWEET VALLEY HIGH gang
* Who's in love . . . and who's not
* What Loveletters fans are saying.

What's New:
* Be on the inside track for upcoming titles

If you don't already receive Loveletters, fill out this coupon, mail it in, and you will receive Loveletters several times a year. Loveletters...you're going to love it!

- -